Fun with Choral Speaking

Fun with Choral Speaking

Rose Marie Anthony

1990
Teacher Ideas Press
A Division of
Libraries Unlimited, Inc.
Englewood, Colorado

TEACHER IDEAS PRESS
A Division of Libraries Unlimited, Inc.
P.O. Box 3988
Englewood, CO 80155-3988

Library of Congress Cataloging-in-Publication Data

Anthony, Rose Marie.
    Fun with choral speaking / Rose Marie Anthony.
    xiv, 138 p. 22x28 cm.
    Includes index.
    Summary: A collection of poetry, aimed at the primary grades,
suitable for choral speaking, and with instructions for a teacher
using the material.
    ISBN 0-87287-773-6
    1. Choral speaking. 2. Choral recitations. 3. Poetry--Study and
teaching (Primary) 4. Children's poetry--Study and teaching
(Primary) 5. Poetry--Collections. 6. Children's poetry.
7. Education, Primary--Activity programs. [1. Poetry--Collections.
2. Nursery rhymes. 3. Choral speaking.] I. Title.
PN4193.C5A57   1990
808.5'5--dc20   90-38877
                                                       CIP
                                                       AC

I dedicate this book

- to my Mom and Dad whom I love very much

- to all poets who write for children

- to the many wonderful children who enjoyed poetry with me over the years

Table of Contents

Part One
Choral Speaking

**Part Two
Mother Goose Rhymes**

Part Three
Poetry Potpourri

Part Four
Appendixes

Acknowledgments

Every effort has been made to trace the ownership and obtain the proper reprint permissions for copyrighted material.

We gratefully acknowledge:

Polly Chase Boyden for "Mud." Reprinted by permission of Killian Jordan.

Gwendolyn Brooks, author, for "The Admiration of Willie" and "Andre." Reprinted by permission of the author.

Curtis Brown, Ltd. for "Get 'Em Here" by Lee Bennett Hopkins. Copyright © 1970 by Lee Bennett Hopkins. Used by permission of Curtis Brown, Ltd.

Marchette Chute for "My Dog" from *Around and About* by Marchette Chute. Copyright © 1957 by E. P. Dutton, Inc. Copyright renewed by Marchette Chute, 1985. Reprinted by permission of the author.

William Cole for "News Story" and "Too Sad." Copyright © 1977 by William Cole. Use by permission of the author.

Aileen Fisher for "After a Bath," "Snail's Pace" and "Voice of the Sky." By permission of the author who holds all rights.

Quotation on page xiii is from *Pass the Poetry, Please! : The Revised Edition*, by Lee Bennett Hopkins. Copyright © 1987 by Lee Bennett Hopkins. Reprinted by permission of Harper and Row Publishers, Inc. and Curtis Brown, Ltd.

Bobbi Katz for "Conversation with a Kite" from *Poems for Small Friends* by Bobbi Katz. Copyright © 1989 by Random House, Inc. Bobbi Katz for "Things to Do If You Are a Subway." Copyright © 1970. Used by permission of the author who controls all rights.

Vachel Lindsay for "The Moon's the North Wind's Cooky" from *Collected Poems* by Vachel Lindsay. Courtesy of Macmillan Publishing Company, Inc., 1925.

Ilo Orleans for "I Thank You, God" and "The Frog on the Log." Reprinted by the permission of Karen Solomon.

Emily Oszewski for "Dusting," "Simone (My Cat)" and "Nightfall." Reprinted by permission of the author who controls all rights.

Mary Ellen Paulson for "Teeth" and "Yellow." Used by permission of the author who controls all rights.

Laura E. Richards for "The Baby Goes to Boston" from *Tirra Lirra: Rhymes Old and New*. Courtesy of Little, Brown and Company, Publishers, 1955.

Arnold Spilka for "Hippopotamusses" and "All Dressed Up" from *A Lion I Can Do Without*. Copyright © 1964 Arnold Spilka. All Rights Reserved. Reprinted by permission of Marian Reiner for the author.

William Wise for "Run, Ducks, Run" and "Up a Tree." Reprinted by permission of William Wise. Copyright © 1971 William Wise.

Irene Zimmerman for "Awakening." Permission granted by Franciscan Herald Press. Irene Zimmerman for "Family Tree (An Unsuccessful Falling Out)." Used by permission of the author who holds all rights.

Introduction

Choral speaking dates back to ancient times. It was an artistic form of oral expression that peoples used to entertain in dramatic stage performances and festivals or to inform the public at assemblies or meetings. People also recited psalms and hymns in unison or in antiphon at religious ceremonies. There is a beauty and power dynamic in choral speaking by a large group that cannot be captured in any other verbal way.

While teaching a children's and young adult literature course, I came across a brochure with an excerpt by Lee Bennett Hopkins on it. The quote touched me deeply because I can identify readily with its every word.

> I am a piper of poetry. If it were within my power, I would introduce it to every child. Poetry can work with any grade and any age level. It can meet the interests and abilities of anyone—anywhere—from the gifted to the most reluctant reader. And it can open up worlds to children they never thought possible. But most important, it can be a source of love and hope that children can carry with them the rest of their lives.

Ever since I read this, I like to think of myself as another "piper of poetry." Teaching poetry to young children through the medium of choral speaking has been one of the most exhilarating experiences of my teaching and library careers. I find choral speaking to be a value-packed educational activity that takes but a few moments or minutes a day and reaps so much enthusiasm and pure joy among the children.

The scope of this book covers the kindergarten to third grade audience, but it will also be helpful for people working in intermediate grades who have never been introduced to this oral art in the primary grades. The poetry collection in parts 2 and 3 was chosen with the primary grades in mind, but I believe quality poetry is ageless. Poems appropriate for younger children can always be used with anyone older. That belief does not work in reverse.

I define choral speaking as the oral art of a group sharing poetry by expressively speaking it together for enjoyment. One key element is enjoyment, fun time, entertainment, happy time, or whatever you choose to call it. Somewhere I read that choral speaking is also a "unique social experience." I agree. Unfortunately over the past thirty years, the words "choral speaking" have seldom been heard, and a review of the literature confirms the fact. What I propose to bring about by the use of this book is a new beginning of this oral art by presenting my easy method for beginners—both the children and the adults, who will act as directors or teachers. Throughout this volume, the words director, instructor, leader, teacher, all connote the same person, be it teacher, librarian, camp activity worker, or any other adult serving the young.

By giving children a strong, happy start with this medium of learning poetry, they will grow to love this literary form. The young who have been reared on choral speaking of poetry will be capable of tackling more difficult selections in middle and upper grades through high school and adulthood. Waiting to introduce choral speaking in fourth grade or later is not preferred. By this time the poetry they encounter in reading and language texts is becoming more comprehensive, and the children are more inhibited because of peer pressure. Therefore, I encourage all who work with the primary audience to take up this pleasurable task of aiding children to "feel at home" with poetry.

Thirty years ago, books on choral speaking, few as they were, generally dissected every poem, often line by line, for oral interpretation by the children. If the books were for middle and upper grades, the lines were divided by voice pitch—low, medium, and high. Some lines were reserved for solos. I strongly suspect that the difficulty and technicality of past choral arrangements may have turned teachers and children away from choral speaking altogether.

I think that young children must learn a poem as a whole. They are too eager and too impatient to wait for a line-by-line interpretation. Primary-school children want to do and know things "all by themselves." Even younger children will say, "Me do it!" By introducing whole short poems first in unison, the children will become proficient in engaging in ready recall. Variations in interpretations and simple arrangements can follow. At this young age, the mind memorizes quickly, which makes the director's job easier. Following my rote method, you will be able to share many poems, limericks, Mother Goose rhymes, nonsense ditties, and others without ever mentioning the word "memorize" and certainly never assigning memorization of a poem as homework at this level.

Part 1 deals with the "how to" of choral speaking. It is directed primarily to those who have little or no knowledge of choric speech; however, veterans of the art may enjoy some new insights. I recommend reading this part thoroughly, so you "feel at home" with the whole procedure before attempting to teach any of the selections in the next two parts.

Part 2 is devoted to Mother Goose nursery rhymes, some familiar and some not so familiar. Do not hesitate to use old and unfamiliar alike. Grades two and three will also relish some of the more unfamiliar rhymes while reviewing their old-time kindergarten and first grade favorites. Following each rhyme, I've offered suggestions for use, interpretation, and arrangement. But every user of this book can rely on his or her own creative talents in devising interpretations and arrangements.

Part 3 contains some of my best-loved repertoire, again with interpretations and suggestions. Teach only those pieces that appeal most strongly to you. There is no dirth of excellent poetry available; the hard task is to peruse and choose the very best for choral speaking.

In appendixes A and B, listings of Mother Goose and other collections will aid you in searching out new material. Works of contemporary and past poets are often published in magazines and newspapers for children, teachers, and librarians. Poet and first-line indexes are included for your convenience. Finally, my wish is that you may encounter the pure joy of hundreds of children happily sharing poetry with you because you took time to be a "piper" of the tunes, rhymes, and rhythms of poetry for each of them.

Part One
Choral Speaking

The Benefits of
Choral Speaking

Definition

By writing this book on choral speaking, I envision passing along my love for and fun with poetry to you. My only hope is that you in turn will pass the gift of poetry along to the kindergarten through third grade audiences you meet. You will discover the multifaceted values of choral speaking. Your dedication and engagement in this activity will be rewarded over and over again by children saying, "Let's do that again."

I reiterate my definition of the subject. Choral speaking is the oral art of a group sharing poetry by expressively speaking it together for enjoyment, fun time, recreation.

Voices

The voice is an instrument for both singing and speaking. No one questions the importance and aesthetic beauty of the singing voice. But what about the sheer beauty, melody, and rhythm of the speaking voice? Do we take that for granted? Almost all people of the world use their speaking voices more than their singing voices. Therefore, I feel adults who work with children have an obligation to help them discover and train their speaking voices. I am not referring to ordinary talking which kindergartners and primary-grade children do endlessly, sometimes to our displeasure. I mean a whole-hearted revival of speaking poetry chorally so the young may experience that their voices can jump, dance, hop, skip, bang, shiver, laugh, bump, snort, dart, cry, whisper, ad infinitum.

If this opportunity, to discover their real voices, is denied our young, many children will go through a life time never fully understanding the voice's impact on their lives. The time element for choral speaking is so minimal; the payoff is for life.

Values

Keeping in mind that choral speaking's primary aim is enjoyment and fun—something to lighten the work and tensions of the day's learning—there are also other values, both short and long term.

Choral speaking can nurture an appreciation of poetry among children. Children should never get to fourth grade and say they hate poetry. If they do, someone made them read and memorize poetry before they were ready or they were never properly introduced to the rhythm and rhyme, the words and fun of poetry. Poetry is meant to be heard first, spoken second, and read only when reading skills are sufficiently matured so children can read simple poetry with relative ease.

Other benefits of choral speaking include learning to speak with precise diction, expression, projection, tone, and volume; increasing listening and speaking vocabularies through the wealthy language of poetry; developing aesthetic and emotional acumen by osmosis; and, enlarging basic knowledge by encounters with new experiences as expressed in poetic forms.

Almost every kindergarten and primary-grade class has children who have slight or severe speech problems. Choral speaking activity is good therapy for these children because they hear crisp, oral speech and try to imitate it. Seeing and reading the director's lips is very helpful. Children with speech problems can enjoy poetry by getting caught up in the action of the group and not worrying about how their words sound. They lose their feelings of inhibition and embarrassment. Moreover, all the children feel comfortable with that feeling of belonging to something much larger than themselves.

There is an electrifying dynamic of excitement and togetherness as children engage in choric speech. I feel totally incapable of describing that dynamic. It must be experienced through actual choral speaking involvement.

The electrifying excitement of choric speech was evident during two performances of a ten-minute spot that I directed. The seventy first and second graders performed beyond my wildest expectations. They were so highly group motivated that it was relatively easy to direct that large number and keep them together. The audiences applauded enthusiastically in appreciation of our work and skill, and for the wonderful poetry. For weeks after the program, teachers and parents talked about the choral speaking performance—an activity new to many of them. One mother remarked, "Now I know why Andy says, 'One two, buckle my shoe …' as he puts his shoes on every morning." This rhyme was in our program. The words and rhythms get right in the children's bones and, without help, they can call up a rhyme any time they please.

Developing memory is wisely done at an early age. Television has had a visual and auditory impact on learning. The young readily absorb and imitate what they hear, especially if the material has lively words and strong beats—elements present in some television programs and choral speaking. Dozens of ditties, nonsense rhymes, nature poems, experiential compositions, and others, can be assimilated through repetition.

Memorization from a printed page is a different but necessary kind of memory exercise. Silent seeing and interpretation for meaning is more difficult than aural reception and expressive vocal interpretation. A balance should be the norm.

The values of choric speech reach beyond the grade school. People who are trained in verbal and facial expression will benefit, no matter what occupation or role they enter.

I would like to relate a few personal examples to enhance my point of view about the values of choral speaking. A while back, a mother came up to me at a public function and queried, "Aren't you Sister Rose Marie? My son had you in second grade. Now he's twenty-six and has a six-month old baby of his own. He still remembers 'Jiggle joggle, jiggle joggle' and says it to the baby all the time." Because of the catchy words of this refrain from Laura E. Richards' poem "The Baby Goes to Boston" (p. 64), he never forgot them. The mother and I visited and I gave her the title and author of the poem so she could get a copy of the whole selection from a children's anthology. Of all the things we could have reminisced about, "Jiggle joggle, jiggle joggle" came first to her mind.

Another of my former primary students took the lead in *Carousel* at the Pabst Theater in Milwaukee. Early choral speaking and singing provided her the chance to be on stage as a small child, which gave her a running start. The mother of another former student told me her daughter is studying acting and had played in many productions. She thanked me for the training I had given her in the second grade.

Once I was invited to an eighth-grade class for storyhour (most of these children had been my students in second grade). After a couple of stories, one student asked me if I still remembered the poem about the mice. I started the first line of the poem. The class joined in and we moved right on to two more favorites they still remembered from second grade.

When the senior high was producing *The Sound of Music*, all the grade schools in the city were searched for children to play the ten Von Trapp children. Each child had to sing a song on pitch and say a poem or reading. I coached six children from our school—four second graders and two sixth graders. Of over 100 applicants, four of those I coached were chosen. One boy, who did not receive a part, is now a priest and his choral training should hold him in good stead as he preaches. I have a faint recollection that the girl who was not chosen ended up on the Pabst Theater stage in *Carousel*.

Instruction

The Director

In kindergarten and primary grades, the teacher, librarian or other adult acts as conductor, leader, and interpreter. Expressive interpretation requires "ultimate oomph" on part of the director. You must have a good sense of rhythm, crisp diction, the ability to use appropriate facial and vocal expression, and a happy rapport with the group to be directed. Gentle discipline is a must, not by way of punishment, but by respect for each member of the group. In a sense, the group controls the group.

No two conductors operate with the same style. Feel comfortable with the style that achieves the effect you want in each poem. Conducting, just as for musical groups, means using fingers, hands, arms, eye contact, and facial expressions. Lead the group by indicating the starts, stops, louds, softs, rhythm, mood, and punctuation.

Sharp starts and clean-cut endings in unison are very important. A small movement of the hand controls both. If you are performing a fast-paced piece or have a large group before you, a whole arm slash movement, from head to side, may be needed for a clean-cut ending. Feel your way. Use only enough hand and arm movement necessary to achieve your desired rendition of the selection. Keep the beat and motion for inflections and vocal punctuation, while at the same time indicate volume and/or speed change. A palms-upward movement is excellent for a crescendo and a palms-downward movement works well for diminuendo.

The children will be so intrigued by your hand movements that they will automatically start imitating you. Discourage this immediately. Their hands should rest quietly in their laps, if they are sitting on the floor; on their desks, if they are sitting there; or, at their sides, if they are standing.

The facial and vocal expressions of an excellent conductor are like an electrical charge for the group. Children imitate readily, and you can help them feel a variety of poetic moods—warmth, laughter, quiet, comfort, surprise, anger, joy, disappointment, mystery, meditation, and so on. Sing-song rendition of poetry will be killed outright if the children never hear what it sounds like.

As director, encourage the children to use their whole vocal mechanism when choral speaking. Often remind them that they speak with their *whole mouth*—teeth, tongue, and lips. Over and above, if you are an appropriate model of facial expression of moods, the children will try to imitate. Overexaggeration of facial and vocal expression detracts from the poem. At times, the natural facial expressions of the children are so funny, you may lose control and laugh. Do not let them know why you are laughing because you could destroy their originality.

The spoken voice must be the primary focus; facial appearances are only secondary. Simple actions, such as, clapping, tapping, tongue-clicking, arm, or leg movements, should be used in moderation and should not detract from the spoken word. Since this book is geared for the K-3 grade levels, some poems, such as, "One, Two, Buckle My Shoe" and "Popcorn," can be activity poems. Introduce only a few activity poems each year.

The Children

Usually, K-3 classes contain 20-35 children; however, librarians may have much larger groups for storyhours and the age levels may vary. Small children have tiny voices, but when they are shown how to enunciate and project their voices clearly, volume without strain follows. All groups can produce that togetherness and momentum I spoke of in the section on values. When you are experienced and confident enough, join smaller, trained groups to total 50-70 or more.

As a grade school library coordinator, I have the advantage of meeting all the grades once a week. So from kindergarten to grade three, I work up a wonderful repertoire of choral speaking compositions. After years of training speaking groups, I can combine groups and have a super program for any audience in ten minutes. Children love to perform in all situations. I will talk about programming later.

It might be good here to mention that if third grade children have had training in choral speaking from first grade on, they will be ready to begin some interpretations of the poems near the end of the second semester. In addition, a few might be capable of directing the group. Middle and upper grade students will be more involved in the interpretation and directing of the groups. That is beyond the scope of this book but it gives you some idea of what the children in K-3 are preparing for through choral speaking activity. Hopefully, the choral speaking experience will continue into the intermediate and upper grades. But even if this activity stops after one or two years, the children will have grown immeasurably in love for poetry and voice development.

The Process

Poems are taught in the same manner as a child learns a song by rote. Begin by reciting a short, humorous poem or Mother Goose selection to the whole group. Almost always, some will beg, "Say that again!" Do so. After repetition, invite the children to learn it. One line at a time, say the poem with expression and sharp diction, and have the class repeat. Proceed with you and the children speaking two lines alternately. Finally, recite together all of the lines in sequence, after instructing the children to watch your lips, just in case they are unsure of the words.

Repeat the whole poem two or three times in succession while giving words of praise and motivation as the process continues. If a child loses out on a line one day, the line will be caught on another day. The children need not fear to make a mistake because the whole group will cover for them. Directors make mistakes too. Allow the children to have a laugh on you "once in a blue moon." Directors who make mistakes often are not well prepared.

The attention span of small children is short at ages four and five. In first through third grade the span lengthens. Use small spurts of time and short poems to begin choral speaking activity. Two to five minutes is sufficient time to introduce a two- or five-line poem. Gradually increase the length of your selections. If the poem is comprehensive, do not practice all the verses in one day. In the school setting you have the whole year to begin and develop a group. That thought should be comforting.

Do not set special times for choral speaking. Let it happen. Surprise the children at any time of the day with an invitation to recite a poem they know or to learn a new one. While waiting in line for lunch or dismissal, enjoy a verse or two. It takes but moments.

Integrate choral speaking into math, language, reading, science, religious education, or any subject. Poems will spark up your lessons. The children can learn much from a related rhyme and enjoy it at the same time. Rhymes help them to remember important information. Many times teacher's manual committees have searched out suitable poems for you to use. Librarians have the 800 classified sections to flush out related poems for storyhours. Also, they can help fill your requests.

Since choral speaking is an oral art, a good deal of repetition is needed. Refrain from teaching more than one poem at a time. By year's end, choral groups will have learned many poems for enjoyment. What an accomplishment for both children and director.

Inform the person who will work with your children the next year about their progress in choral speaking. That person might be enticed to continue where you left off. You can be the best salesperson for reviving choral speaking in our nation's schools and libraries. Any interested and capable adult can carry on this recreational activity.

Types of Poetry for Choral Speaking

Some poems fall neatly into one type or category, but others may contain elements of more than one type. The following explanations are generalizations in categorizing children's poetry.

Poems in Unison

Any poem may be learned in unison by all the children learning and saying the entire rhyme together. Introduce almost every number in this manner. Unison recitation provides powerful, strong renditions. Poems children especially like are fun when spoken in unison. It is profitable to begin choral speaking using poems with strong beats, nonsense words, and/or humor. The introduction to this activity will determine how well the children get caught up in the experience. Keep in mind that you are developing and training a choral group; therefore, on some numbers, variety in simple arrangements is your goal after unison practice is completed. But some well-chosen selections will remain permanent unison pieces in your repertoire.

Poems with Refrains or Antiphons

Refrain compositions are often lengthy and tell a substantial tale. But because of repetitious lines they are fairly easy to perform. Normally the adult leader will convey the story line while the whole group or groups come in on the refrain lines. An antiphon usually pertains to a composition of a religious nature, such as a psalm, hymn, or canticle; however, it is performed in the same way as a refrain. Adaptations or simplified versions of biblical psalms or narrative passages are suitable for K-3 children.

As third graders mature in choral speaking, they (or one child) with clear expressive voices, can read the narrative parts of a refrain or antiphonal selection. The teacher may join the refrain group. Some examples are: "The Baby Goes to Boston," Laura E. Richards (p. 64); "A Farmer Went Trotting," Mother Goose (p. 30); and, "Keeper of the Sheep," Rose Marie Anthony (p. 74).

Poems for Dialogue

The words of dialogue poems clearly define their type. Most always, two persons or things are carrying on the conversation throughout. Natural, expressive, conversational speech is apropos. Numerous dialogue poems are short; start with these. Lengthier dialogue poetry is more aptly performed by experienced choric groups.

Various groupings may alternate speaking the lines: girls and boys; teacher and children; or two solos. Sometimes two sides of the room or two rows of children can carry on the talk. Examples include "Pussy Cat, Pussy Cat," Mother Goose (p. 45); "Chick, Chick, Chatterman," Mother Goose (p. 25); "Family Tree (An Unexpected Falling Out)," Irene Zimmerman (p. 81); "Merry Sunshine," Anonymous (p. 114); and, "Whistle, Daughter, Whistle," Mother Goose (p. 48).

Poems of Sequence

Sequence poems adapt conveniently to one line per child. Each line is a complete thought, often, but not necessarily, punctuated as separate sentences. This type of arrangement is the hardest to vocalize, as each child must come in precisely on the beat without interrupting the rhythm. Tackle the one-line-per-child arrangement only with experienced groups.

Teach this type of poem in unison or group arrangements first, then, after much practice, try the one-line-per-child recitation. You may be pleasantly surprised at the outcome. It is good for the group to listen to others speak their lines. Dwelling on compositions of this type too long, however, will cause the children to become restless.

Poems suitable for sequence recitation are: "Timbuctoo," Marchette Chute (p. 59); "There Was a Crooked Man," Mother Goose (p. 44); "Pussy Willow Song," American folk song (p. 94); and, "Taking Off," Anonymous (p. 92).

Poems of Cumulation

Cumulative poems have repetitious lines to which a new line is added after each verse. "There Was an Old Lady Who Swallowed a Fly" (p. 106) is an example. This type of poetry becomes quite long as the lines accumulate, but the children do not mind. They relish the repetitious challenge that taxes their memories and vocal output. Sometimes these lines become tongue twisters, depending on the speed with which you move the group. Unison recitation is not fitting because the children will peter out. Try groups reciting lines so the children have a chance to rest their voices.

Some cumulative selections are: "The House That Jack Built," Mother Goose; "What Did You Put in Your Pocket?," by Beatrice Schenk deRegniers from *Juba This and Juba That*; and, "The Twelve Days of Christmas," a traditional Christmas song.

See appendixes A and B for collections that include these cumulative poems.

Poems for Activity

Activity poems for choral speaking are my creation. Some may disagree that activity poems are choral speaking, but my point of view differs when considering the age group with which you are working. Certain selections are best suited for recitation with activity. Carefully chosen, these are the only poems where the activity is of equal importance to the oral rendition.

"The Grand Old Duke of York" (p. 32) or "One, Two, Buckle My Shoe" (p. 43) are examples of activity poems for choral speaking. True, they can be just choral pieces, and should first be taught as choral pieces. But they also serve as superb movement or wiggle-time selections, especially for K-2. Bring this poetry to the playground at recess time, also. In parts 2 and 3 you will locate some rhymes of this type and suggested actions for use. Make up other actions for these and some different poems you place in your own personal collection.

Choral activity poems include: "Funny Bunny," Rose Marie Anthony (p. 82); "Pussy Willow Song," American folk song (p. 94); and, "Jack Be Nimble," Mother Goose (p. 33).

Do not incorporate action into every choral piece. Action throughout a choral number is limited to a minimal group of activity poems. In some selections, minimal activity may be used to enhance a climax or a particular line. These are not considered activity poems. During a performance, activity rhymes can be spoken without movement if you lack space.

Poems to Solo

A solo is counted as a group of one, as in math. Often poems express one child's feelings about a certain subject. On occasion, individual children may be invited to recite a short selection of this kind for the class or a performance. Even though the whole group knows the rhyme, they should be taught to respect and listen to one another quietly. Over time, give all an opportunity to solo. If a child refuses, so be it. To force a child would be disastrous. Some children, like some adults, are not cut out for solo performance, but each child is a valuable member of your choral group. If a reluctant child asks to be a solo, oblige readily before there is a change of mind.

Selections appropriate for solo poems are: "Too Sad," William Cole (p. 62); "Andre," Gwendolyn Brooks (p. 83); "I Thank You God," Ilo Orleans (p. 84); "Awakening," Irene Zimmerman (p. 109); and, "Something about Me," Anonymous (p. 88).

I want to clarify that any short poem can be performed as a solo, even though its content does not speak from the point of view of one child. In the same vein, any poem with solo content may be vocalized by the whole group. The word "solo" also refers to single solo lines spoken in any given choral recitation. For performances in a large auditorium, a solo child should use a microphone so the voice is not strained and all the words are heard.

Sometimes characteristics of more than one type of poem are present in a selection. This poses no problem for the director. It is helpful to be aware of this when planning a program containing a variety of selections.

Keeping Arrangements Simple

Groupings

In examining the few choral speaking books of the past that I could find, I am frustrated that often every line was assigned to a group, solo, or row, etc. Frequently, the sense of the lines was chopped into pieces by these groupings. Choral speaking must have become a chore and a bore. I have often wondered if choral speaking activity discontinued in schools and libraries many years ago because the arrangements became so technical.

In the past, choral speaking groups were divided by speaking voice — light, medium, and dark; or, high, medium, and low (similar to soprano, alto, and bass in singing groups). I do not advocate any division of kindergarten to third grade children by voice pitch. By fourth grade, students' voices are more developed for assignment to a pitch group.

People who use my book with intermediate-grade children who have never been introduced to choral speaking might try at least a semester of fun with my easy method before attempting voice pitch grouping. See the end pages of May Hill Arbuthnot's *Time for Poetry*. She offers excellent help to intermediate-grade teachers and librarians by suggesting ways to divide children into pitch groups.

In this book, groupings may vary: girls — boys; teacher — children; group one — group two; row one — row two — row three; three groupings of five. ALL stands for the total group. SOLO is considered a group of one. Multiple groupings are possible for any chosen piece. One of the director's most important jobs is to determine *who* will say *what* lines.

Arrangements

Initially, the easiest types of poetry to work with are unison, dialogue, refrain, or activity poems. Teach beginners many of these selections in the early months. Short poems are great to start recitation in unison. All learn the lines together, so they have a total sense of the given composition. Later, experiment with simple choral arrangements. This can be done the same day, especially if the children are catching on fast and are intrigued with the piece. Wait until another day if you or they are tired. I will not give specific examples of arrangements here as parts 2 and 3 present detailed explanations. Occasionally teach a sequence poem in unison in the first semester. When the children have a good hold on the words and the process, begin one-line-per-child or solo assignments.

Punctuation is a fitting help as you decide what groupings seem feasible. At times, two lines or a line-and-a-half are recited before a natural pause at a comma or period occurs; other times, a quotation may run two or three lines or more. It is more natural for one person or a group to say the whole quote than to divide the lines for two or three solos.

Refrain lines are often spoken by all if the refrain requires zip and volume. On the other hand, in a quiet selection, a solo or a very small group could echo the refrain. Most children's poems that are classified as dialogue poems are conversations between two persons or things. Therefore, it makes sense that only two groups (one of which could be a solo) are needed.

As an observant and understanding director, you will know when children are ready for more advanced arrangements. You will, as I have, make mistakes. The children's renditions will let you know when you are attempting something too hard. Occasionally, challenge them to something harder, so you will know what they can perform. *Know the capabilities of your group.* And then use your best judgment.

As I said before, the individual rhymes in this collection have specific arrangements for experimentation. But no group designations are typed in the poem copy. I purposely avoided doing this so you can decide how you want to interpret your selections. No two or ten conductors will arrange and speak any choral selection the same way. That is the wonder of this fun-loving activity called choral speaking.

Programming

Programs should be an outgrowth of class enjoyment of poetry. Your time spent on choral speaking should not be solely to prepare for a program. Once you and the children have had a full measure of enjoyment, however, the only proper thing to do is share that joy with others.

Choral speaking opportunities get to a point where "the cup runneth over." Audiences can be classes within the school building, visitors to the school or library, parents, neighbors, the public, etc. If you travel from room to room, like troubadours, visit only a few classes a day so the children do not tire.

Take advantage of impromptu opportunities to share poetry. Ask library visitors if they have time for a rhyme. The children can perform three poems of medium length in approximately a minute or more. Should you be going on a nature or exercise walk with a group of choral speakers, offer a poem or two to some of the passersby. The oral tradition of storytelling has made a strong comeback over the past several years. I hope the oral tradition of reciting poetry aloud for entertainment can be revived.

One caution: do not allow anyone to pressure you into doing a program for every occasion. Poems need to be absorbed slowly with much repetition and over a long period of time. Refuse short notices to perform so children will not force-learn rhymes. Plan months ahead if you choose to do a program or if you suspect you will be asked to do one.

A variety of the poetry types—unison, dialogue, refrain, etc.—should be represented in a program. Include slow, fast, and moderate numbers with differing moods. Avoid the mistake of reciting every poem the children ever learned, unless they are beginners with a small repertoire.

Choral speaking is not dramatics or theatrics. No costumes, props, or special lighting are needed. All these embellishments detract and distract from the poetry. Microphones are not needed unless the group is small, the hall is large, or the acoustics are poor. You might need a microphone for solos.

Avoid overpractice. When working with the group of seventy first and second graders, mentioned previously, we had one eight-and-a-half-minute practice on the stage. That was the length of our program and it included ten selections.

Should you as conductor make a mistake while directing and the result is gobbledegook, stop immediately. Do not try to pull the children through to the end. Simply turn to the audience, tell them you made a mistake and start over. When a child makes a mistake, it usually does not throw the whole group off. Do try for an excellent performance but do not allow yourself to be annoyed if a mistake happens. The audience will be so charmed at the children's performance they will hardly be aware of a mistake.

Throughout the program, a director's voice must never be heard above that of the children. Speak softly or guide the children with lip movements just to get them started. When well trained, the children will not need much verbal help. Any performance on stage needs a director throughout the program. Do not abandon the children through a sense of timidity or fear. Director and choral group are a team that play together. Also, to avoid distracting the children, do not wear sparkly, light-catching jewelry when you are conducting.

Elements of Poetry

I have chosen to discuss three elements of poetry that pertain to choral speaking: language, rhythm, and mood. Knowledge of these three elements is basic to understanding choral speech. There are more elements of poetry but they are beyond the scope of this book.

Language

The poignant, precise, often vigorous words of poetic language reinforce meanings and concepts for the child, even though some words may be unfamiliar. Through the aural and oral experiences of choral speaking, children imbibe an inner awareness of the words of language which can explode, dance, run, jump, hop, and jog. Words can also be slow, smooth, gentle, brief, musical, lilting, and so forth.

Poets "pressure pack" their words and concepts by creating rhymes with not one unnecessary word. They convey their experiences, imaginative thoughts, and laughter in poems that I compare to value packs offering "more for your money" at the store. A well-chosen rhyme gives you more for your time and effort when reading and sharing it with children. All the following examples of language of poetry are taken from the collection in parts 2 and 3.

Consider the words, "The Moon's the North Wind's Cooky" (p. 60), "treetops autumn-thinned" (p. 86), and, "wiggly mud" (p. 97). They stretch the mind to see familiar things in a more dressed-up way. You will discover numerous value packs in this collection as well as in any poem book you read.

Consonants have crisp sounds like *t* and *k*; hummy sounds like *m* and *n*; heavy sounds like *b, d, g, j*; breathy sounds like *h* and *p*. Listen! The cuckoo clock goes "tick-a-tock-a, tick-a-tock-a." In "The Baby Goes to Boston,"

Laura Richard's train travels "Jiggle joggle, jiggle joggle" (p. 64). The light-hearted fairy "dances and sings to the sound of its wings, with a hey and a heigh and a ho!" (p. 78). The puffs of air needed to pronounce the *h* sounds make you feel like the tiny fairy is being blown lightly from "hey" to "heigh" to "ho" on each puff of breath.

Consonant blends and digraphs also provide many a poet with enticing words for children. For fun try the following: "Whiskey, whaskey, weedle" (p. 42); "Spring is showery, flowery, bowery" (p. 50); and, Laura Richard's masterful tongue twister, "Loky, moky, poky, stoky, smoky, choky, chee!" (p. 64). Children are verbally challenged by the last refrain since that train is going full speed ahead. It takes a while, but a good conductor will help the children master the twister with numerous repetitions over many days.

Vowel sounds, too, including the vowel digraphs and murmur dipthongs, make up part of the language of poetry. In Lear's bear limerick (p. 103) I interpret the short *o* as *ah*, a happy sound. Four repetitious short *o* sounds in "Moppsikon, Floppsikon bear," in conjunction with the nonsensical meaning, produce a feeling of joyous disbelief in the reciter. The selection, "The Squirrel," (p. 90) has words like, "Snappity crackity," "Whirly twirly," and "Furly curly," that add vocal and aural delight to choral articulation. One of Mother Goose's seasonal rhymes calls autumn, "wheezy, sneezy, freezy" (p. 50). The long *e* sounds make it easy to wrinkle up your nose as if ready to sneeze.

Repetitious letter sounds or alliteration at the beginnings of words are fun for children to vocalize: "Chick, chick, chatterman," (p. 25) "Bumpety, bumpety, bump" (p. 30), and "diddle, diddle" (p. 28). The centipede "lay *di*stracted in a *di*tch" (p. 105), shows another way sounds are repeated.

Rhyme is the part of language that tickles our ears. Miss Tuckett sitting "on a bucket," (p. 38) Michael Finnegan "wearing his whiskers on his chinnegan" (p. 36), popcorn going "hop, hop, hop" and "pop, pop, pop" (p. 87) are unforgettable. Rhyme haunts the memory. It is this haunting element of language that makes poetry easy to memorize and quick to recall. I cannot stress enough what a grand gift you give to children when you steep their memories full of rhymes. For years to come, daily humdrum or surprise experiences will trigger a recalled rhyme to share with others or enjoy just by oneself—that is built-in entertainment.

You cannot direct children to speak naturally if they are forced to pronounce words awkwardly, rather than comfortably in their own dialect. In a section on choral speaking in her book *Children's Literature in the Elementary School* (see appendix C for complete citation), Charlotte Huck cautions choral directors to use word pronunciations from the part of the country in which they teach. I agree. If you listen to tapes or recordings of poetry to seek out new material for your choral groups, adapt pronunciations to suit your region.

Rhythm

Second to rhyme, rhythm implants poems right into our bones and bodies. You feel the multiple rhythms when chorally reciting verses. There is no getting away from it.

I define "beat" as the accented syllables in each line of a rhyme. The rhythm might be described as the overall flow—the crescendos, decrescendos, inflections, expressions, and, interpretations the choral director renders in the chorus piece.

In the following activity the beat and the rhythm must blend beautifully together. The distinction between the two can be a ticklish problem. When interpreting a poem by the beat alone, a sing-song performance will result. In sing-song, there is an even up-down movement of the voice from beginning to end. For example, say the following in sing-song fashion and listen for the monotonous up-down voice pattern.

<u>Mary</u> <u>had</u> a <u>little</u> <u>lamb</u>,

Its <u>fleece</u> was <u>white</u> as <u>snow</u>.

And <u>everywhere</u> that <u>Mary</u> <u>went</u>

The <u>lamb</u> was <u>sure</u> to <u>go</u>.

Slower verses are more apt to become sing-song if the director does not move the group along at a comfortable talking pace to fit the overall mood. It is extremely boring to listen to a group of spirited, young children perform in a sing-song manner. Sing-song can put both children and the audience to sleep.

In dancing a polka or the twist, you cannot divorce the beat of the music from the rhythmical movement and sway of the dancers. The same is true with choral speaking. Expressive speech in pieces of poetry with very strong beats like, "Popcorn" (p. 87) and "The Grand Old Duke of York" (p. 32), will automatically produce a pop, pop, popping or march, march, marching rhythm. This is not to be confused with sing-song. Rather, it is capturing the mood of the selection. The beat in "Mary Had a Little Lamb" has no comparison in strength with that of these other two selections.

For effect, poets write certain rhymes with dramatic shifts of beat and rhythm. "Taking Off" (p. 92) is a good example. Each line builds in volume with a rhythmical upward movement to the climax. The last line has an abrupt change, both in volume and speed. "The Big Clock" (p. 66) is another selection with two rhythms and beats; one for the big clock, the other for the cuckoo clock.

When teaching pieces in unison like "In a Dark, Dark Wood" (p. 51) or "Yellow" (p. 77), by Mary Ellen Paulson, the repetition of the words in each line will make for monotonous rhythm unless you capture a mood to enhance the words. In the first selection, think spooky; in "Yellow," think of a bright recitation. Dividing into groups will also help the repetitious words come alive. Save pieces of this kind until the children have some experience in choral activity.

Children are apt to latch onto choral speaking more readily if you begin with simple rhymes that have strong rhythms. Try "Popcorn" (p. 87), "I Know a Man Named Michael Finnegan" (p. 36), "Hickory, Dickory, Dock" (p. 26), and "Funny Bunny" (p. 82). For some poems in this collection, specific helps are provided for establishing rhythm. Basically, you must "feel" your own way and define a suitable delivery.

Mood

Mood is that deep, personal, feeling response produced by contact with a poem. I have discussed how the language and rhythm are integral to poetry. The feeling element that poems so lavishly bestow is "the frosting on the cake"—different flavors for different tastes. Each child's likes, dislikes, and experiences at home, at school, with friends, in the city, or the country, will change the flavor of a single rhyme.

William Cole's "News Story" (p. 95) evokes a chuckle at a name like Peter Lumpkin and the reality of that lost tooth. Most identify with the quarter under the pillow (or some other amount). Many will understand and enjoy the exaggeration in knocking out the other teeth to get more money; others interpreting literally, will be shivering at the thought. If a child has just had some painful dental work performed, this hilarious piece may conjure up hurtful memories. A short discussion may be profitable. The director has the best part—seeing all those toothless grins.

"Andre," by Gwendolyn Brooks (p. 83), is a beautiful, sensitive dream sequence about a child and his or her parents. Most children will identify happily with the poem. You may have a child in your group though, whose experience with parents is alcohol, drugs, divorce, or sex abuse. The dream element in this rhyme can be soothing momentarily in this child's life. The thought of actually choosing another mother or father may be comforting. Teachers are at an advantage in knowing more about the personal backgrounds of their group. Librarians and other choral leaders may not be quite so informed. Be sensitive to the kids.

And so, dealing with mood in poetry prompts very personal responses. Explore poetry of many moods with young children so they own a wealth of rhymes, their favorites and not-so-favorites. The following is a short list of titles with moods to experience.

"Things to Do If You Are a Subway" by Bobbi Katz (p. 67)
(noisy, speedy, aggressive)
"Sleep, Baby, Sleep," an old German lullaby (p. 69)
(peaceful, restful, tranquil)
"Mud" by Polly Chase Boyden (p. 97)
(playful, pondering, ecstatic)
"A Centipede" by an unknown author (p. 105)
(happiness, teasing, puzzlement)
"My Dog" by Marchette Chute (p. 111)
(love, friendship, mischievousness)
"Snail's Pace" by Aileen Fisher (p. 72)
(slow, burdensome, tempered with humor)
"The Frog on the Log" by Ilo Orleans (p. 70)
(playful, fearful, grateful)

Poetry Material

Well-selected poems are precious gifts. The inner richness of poetry comes partly from the variety of material available — Mother Goose Rhymes, nonsense verses, realistic poems, religious selections, and so forth. In this section I describe briefly some of the materials you will find in this collection and elsewhere.

Nursery Rhymes — Mother Goose

Mother Goose Nursery rhymes cover a wide range of language, some familiar, some not so familiar. The rhythms vary also, often with emphasis on strong beats. Innumerable moods are explored. Paul Hazard says Mother Goose rhymes have a "magic quality" and I believe, through my experience with them, that that magic casts a spell over all childlike persons — young, middle-aged or autumn-aged.

Most of these collected rhymes are of English origin although some of the earliest American Mother Goose rhymes were fashioned by the first settlers. There also are Chinese Mother Goose rhymes. Every country has ditties of this nature that rise from the oral tradition of the people, but are not necessarily called "Mother Goose."

Often slight or not so slight changes in the words of these rhymes are found as you peruse different collections. When I discover these variations, I choose the version that appeals most to me for choral enjoyment.

Nonsense Verses

Nothing tickles the funny bones of children like nonsense verse. There is something so delicious about rhymes expressing impossibilities that we can never eat enough of them to fill our satisfaction. Humorist John Billings, a contemporary of Abraham Lincoln, said "Good nonsense is good sense in disguise." I hope to remember that always when dealing with children and adults. It is said that humans are distinguished from other creatures by their ability to laugh. Nonsense or topsy-turvy verses are laughter releasers. Especially today, when heavy burdens weigh on small shoulders, adults can help relieve some of the tension through laughter. Masters of nonsense verse are Laura E. Richards, William Cole, David McCord, Ogden Nash, Arnold Spilka, and others.

Humorous Poetry

Humorous poems are funny and very possible. The human condition and the lives of all creatures, animate and inanimate, are subjects for creative humorists to explore and exploit. All poets are masters of observation. I know of no children's poet who writes without humor, however subtle at times. Some express the gift to a greater degree than others but all share humorous insights with their young audiences.

Realistic Poems

The subject matter of reality or being is unquenchable. It must be frustrating for poets to be inspired or at times bombarded with imaginative ideas and not have sufficient time to crack the meanings open in poignant, realistic verse. Poetry is a far more taxing and time-consuming form of writing than prose. We are fortunate indeed that artistic writers of verse pass out their innermost feelings on reality through their writings.

Do keep in mind, however, that young children may not always have had every realistic experience the author talks about. Simple explanations or brief discussions may either precede or follow a choric selection. Avoid meaning overkill! Possibly one day, a similar experience will pounce upon a child's memory and break open the fullest meaning of a poem learned long ago. That happening will be a poetic revelation. In the meantime, the children can enjoy the other elements of poetry—the words, the rhyme, and the rhythm.

Nature Rhymes

Because children are fascinated by things of nature, nature rhymes are included as a separate category, even though they fall into other categories. The littlest are enthralled by anything small enough to fit in the palms of their hands or stuff in their pockets—ants, caterpillars, stones, sticks, grass, leaves, acorns, seeds, etc. As children grow and have more experiences they become more aware of larger realities in nature—animals, plants, trees, water, wind, rain, thunder, lightning, etc. I know of no subject listed here that has not been treated by the poetic pen over and over. Children's poets are truly children's friends.

Aesthetic Verses

Aesthetic verse is artistic, poignant, and discriminative. A selection of this kind will cast an awe experience over you. You will be compelled to read or hear it over and over again. You may want to share it with someone or savor it for yourself alone. Aesthetic compositions contain exceptional language, a glorious, somber, or other flow, without sharply marked rhythm. They capitalize on drawing you into a mood-feeling response. Poems of this category require more astute understanding and are therefore best introduced after children have a hold on rhymes of other types, such as those with strong rhythms, humor, and reality.

Part Two
Mother Goose Rhymes

Chick, Chick, Chatterman

Chick, chick, chatterman

    How much are your geese?

Chick, chick, chatterman

    Five cents a piece.

Chick, chick, chatterman

    That's too dear.

Chick, chick, chatterman

    Get out of here.

"Chick, Chick, Chatterman" is a dialogue poem with a nonsense refrain line that adds a humorous element. In this bargaining situation, the buyer disagrees with the price. This should be reflected in the buyer's voice in line six. The farmer, on the other hand, is certain a fair price has been proffered. Line eight, therefore, calls for an angry tone.

Once the children have memorized the poem, try this arrangement. ALL say the chick, chick lines. Group One or a SOLO is the buyer and will say lines two and six. Group Two or another SOLO is the farmer and will say lines four and eight.

Sometimes the teacher can be the SOLO farmer and pretend to chase the children with a pitchfork or barn broom on the last line. The screaming children will run to the four corners of the room. Inevitably they will beg, "Let's do that again." Outdoors is a great place to play out this rhyme over and over again.

Hickory, Dickory, Dock

Hickory, dickory, dock,

The mouse ran up the clock.

The clock struck one.

The mouse ran down.

Hickory, dickory, dock.

The catchy sound of "Hickory, Dickory, Dock" quickly grabs the children's attention. Try moderate speed. Pronounce all the consonants crisply. It helps to think of a metronome marking four beats to each line to get the feel of the clock ticking. To attain four beats, say the *ck* on the fourth beat.

Hickory	dickory	do-----*ck*
The mouse	ran up the	clo-----*ck*

Consider lines three and four as one line.

The clock	struck one	The mouse	ran down
Hickory	dickory	do-----*ck*	

After the children learn the rhyme in unison, show them how to click their tongues against the roofs of their mouths. Most have no difficulty with this, however, some may need coaching. You can divide the children into BOYS and GIRLS, one group saying the words and the other clicking tongues in perfect timing, four clicks per line. The last click should be made simultaneously with the last *ck* on dock. It may take a few tries to achieve that clear cut off.

For a line progression, ALL could recite lines one and five with SOLOS taking the middle three lines.

One Day a Boy Went Walking

One day a boy went walking

And walked into a store.

He bought a pound of sausage meat

And laid it on the floor.

The boy began to whistle—

He whistled up a tune,

And all the little sausages

Danced around the room.

The nonsense content assures the children's enjoyment of this ditty. Attempt to get the feel of the sausage dance into your recitation by using a fairly marked beat. Pick out words to accent—sausage, all, whistled, danced—whatever sounds right to you. Accent them by raising the voice. Blow on the *wh*'s while maintaining the beat. It is fun to act out this rhyme with all the children acting like sausages. Choose a child to be the buyer. (If you choose a girl, substitute the words "girl" and "she" where necessary.) ALL recite in unison. The instructor, and anyone who can whistle, should whistle the fifth and sixth lines. Decide ahead of time what tune you will whistle. The children pop up off the floor and have a "mini ball" as they sing out the last two lines.

Hey, Diddle, Diddle

Hey, diddle, diddle,

The cat and the fiddle,

The cow jumped over the moon;

The little dog laughed

To see such sport,

And the dish ran away with the spoon.

"Hey, Diddle, Diddle" is a Mother Goose favorite. Try a rhythm of two beats for lines one, two, four, and five. Tap three counts for lines three and six. The extra syllables in line six will require speeding up, which compliments the words "ran away."

<u>And the dish</u>   <u>ran away</u>   <u>with the spoon</u>

Let the children capitalize on the cow mooing on "moon." Just draw the "moo" out a little.

Because there are many *d* words in the beginning, middle, and ending positions of the words, this rhyme could be helpful for phonics. Introduce it when teaching the initial *d* sound; review it again when presenting the end and medial *d* sounds.

The North Wind Doth Blow

The north wind doth blow,

And we shall have snow,

And what will poor robin do then,

Poor thing?

He'll sit in a barn,

And keep himself warm,

And hide his head under his wing,

Poor thing.

This dialogue poem should be rendered in a sympathetic mood. Lines one and two can be verbalized in a matter-of-fact way. On lines three and four a sad facial expression will move the children to express the sense of the lines properly. Elevate with a questioning voice on the words "then" and "thing." Lines five, six, and seven could be voiced in a comforting way with a slight pause after the word "wing." Resume a sad face while reciting the end line with a minimal pause between the words. Children often do not render the *oo* sound correctly. The word "poor" should not sound like "pore" which rhymes with "more."

This rhyme can be grouped in several ways. One group can ask the question; another can answer. Just to be different, two groups can face each other as if in conversation. The teacher can be one of the groups (or a SOLO). Varying line arrangements are viable, also.

A Farmer Went Trotting

A farmer went trotting

Upon his gray mare;

    Bumpety, bumpety, bump!

With his daughter behind him,

So rosy and fair;

    Lumpety, lumpety, lump!

A raven cried "Croak"

And they all tumbled down;

    Bumpety, bumpety, bump!

The mare broke her knees

And the farmer his crown;

    Lumpety, lumpety, lump!

The mischievous raven

Flew laughing away;

    Bumpety, bumpety, bump!

And vowed he would serve them

The same next day;

    Lumpety, lumpety, lump!   BUMP!

In this piece, the farmer and his daughter are having a bad time with the mischievous raven. At a galloping rhythm, the director can recite all narrative lines while the children speak the refrain lines. A low voice pitch and hard *b* sounds on all "bump" lines will add contrast if the "lump" lines are said on a high falsetto tone. The *l* sounds should trip lightly off the end of the tongue. You may have a case of the class giggles on your hands as this sounds so silly. Boys can recite the "bump" lines and girls the "lump" lines or vice versa.

Once mastered, second or third grade leaders can perform the narrative lines as soloists. The teacher can just relax or join in on one of the refrain groups. Another possibility is having a row or group arrangement for the younger children. Many groupings can be experimented with for fun.

For additional enjoyment, one extra "BUMP" can be added as shown in the last line. That is especially effective if the children are sitting at their desks or tables because they can bang their fists once on the surface in unison as the big "BUMP" is said. Children get so caught up in this last movement that they can hurt their hands by banging too hard.

The Grand Old Duke of York

The grand old Duke of York,

He had ten thousand men;

He marched them up to the top of the hill

And he marched them down again.

And when they were up, they were up,

And when they were down, they were down;

And when they were only halfway up,

They were neither up nor down.

"The Grand Old Duke of York" is a precision piece throughout. When introducing this rhyme, show the children how to pitch the voice low and deep while making the voice march in staccato beat and projecting all beginning, medial and final consonant sounds. Wherever the words "up," "down," and "halfway up" appear, they will determine the inflection of the voice pitch. Because of the up-down inflections and the meticulous beat, be well prepared before you start to teach this poem.

After the group learns the selection, vigorous action can accompany the words. Have the children begin in a squatting position, hands on knees. Begin reciting lines one and two. On line three, have them rise up a little on each beat to an upright position by the time you reach the word "hill." (Hands are no longer on knees.) Start the descent on line four back to the squatting position with hands on knees. Have the children stand up quickly on the last word in line five and stay standing through line six with a speedy squat on the last "down." Line seven requires a semi-squatting position. The tension will be great at this point, so allow the children to jump up high with hands stretched upward on "up." Then they can fall down precipitously on the word "down." They will be helter-skelter over the floor.

Use this activity rhyme in unison. For programming, two groups of BOYS (or BOYS and GIRLS) could recite every other two lines with or without actions.

Jack Be Nimble

Jack be nimble,

Jack be quick,

Jack jump over

    The candlestick.

Jump it lively,

Jump it quick,

But don't knock over

    The candlestick.

The very words call for action. An action game can be prepared by covering a suitably sized cardboard tube with heavy cloth, felt, or contact paper to make "candles." A piece of rope or other raffia can be the wick. Jumping candles of varying lengths can be a challenge for the children. When using taller lengths, sort the kids by leg length.

Most children will know the first verse, but verse two may be unfamiliar to many. Practice unison recitation. When the lines are mastered, invite the children to play the game by lining up. Explain that instead of the word "Jack," they will all call out the name of the child whose turn it is to jump. The child whose name is called runs and jumps over the candlestick. So the rest of the line does not get restless, use verse one only. Gradually, a child can jump on each verse. The child who jumps on verse two will not have his or her name called.

If the group is too big, divide the children into two or more groups. One group can play "Jack Be Nimble" while the others engage in another game or task. Volunteer parents could make your candles. Play the game indoors or outdoors.

Intery, Mintery

Intery, mintery, cuttery corn,

Apple seed and apple thorn;

Wine, brier, limber lock,

Three geese in a flock,

One flew east, one flew west,

And one flew over the goose's nest.

Children relish the first three lines of nonsense words simply for the rhyme, repetition, and alliteration. The last three lines make some sense and have a wonderful flow in construction.

If you desire a bit of action, ALL can turn heads to the right in line five on "One flew east"; then ALL can turn heads to the left on "one flew west." Fold hands flat, as if in prayer, and keep them together. The joined hands become the last goose which will rise up and arch off to the right until the end.

Thirty Days Hath September

Thirty days hath September,

April, June, and November,

All the rest have thirty-one,

Excepting February alone,

And that has twenty-eight days clear

And twenty-nine in each leap year.

Learning this poem will help children remember the number of days in each month. I do not like the flow or rhythm in this rhyme but I teach it anyway for the information. This is an exception to my usual position: "Refrain from teaching a poem that does not have strong appeal for you." Do your best to render a pleasing recitation.

Michael Finnegan

I know a man named Michael Finnegan—

He wears his whiskers on his chinnegan.

Along came a wind and blew them in again;

Poor old Michael Finnegan.

Michael Finnegan is a favorite with children. If the group accents each beat with their voices, the words sound like a rousing cheer. Try four beats to the first three lines and three beats to the last line.

I <u>know</u> a <u>man</u> named <u>Mi</u>chael <u>Fin</u>negan—

He <u>wears</u> his <u>whiskers</u> <u>on</u> his <u>chin</u>negan.

A<u>long</u> came a <u>wind</u> and <u>blew</u> them <u>in</u> again;

<u>Poor</u> old <u>Mi</u>chael <u>Fin</u>negan.

Since the *wh* and *w* sounds are different, pronounce the *wh* as a powerful blowing sound. The digraph is not voiced as the *w* in "wear." Direct the children to raise their voice pitch on each of the first four syllables in the last line and then to come down on the last three syllables of that line. It makes a funny climax.

Children will say this ditty over and over again without tiring. For variation, use this selection as a sequence poem—one line per child or group. Try three SOLOS on the first three lines and ALL come in on the last line. Have fun!

Hickle Them, Pickle Them

Hickle them, pickle them,

Catch them and tickle them;

I'll teach the villains to eat my fine pears!

Gobble them, hobble them,

Snatch them and bobble them,

Till all of them fancy they've fallen downstairs.

The funny words in this selection from Mother Goose tickle the children's funny bones. With gusto attack the first two lines and lines four and five with two pronounced beats per line. The owner of the pear tree will get revenge on the children who are stealing his yellow, juicy pears. Lines three and six are lengthy but fit neatly into four metered counts per line.

I'll teach	the villains	to eat my	fine pears
Till all of them	fancy	they've fallen	downstairs

Because of the repetitious sounds and rhymed words, pay extra attention to enunciation. Your efforts in this regard will perk up this composition and make it pleasing to the ears, not to mention the funny bones.

When allotting the lines, keep couplet parts together; perhaps GIRLS on one set and BOYS on the other. Lines three and six lend rightly to a SOLO. A small select group could convey those lines as well.

Little Miss Tuckett

Little Miss Tuckett

Sat on a bucket,

Eating some peaches and cream.

There came a grasshopper

That tried hard to stop her,

But she said, "Go away, or I'll scream."

Little Miss Tuckett is a tough little girl who will not allow a tiny grasshopper to frighten her away. The line pattern is set up the same way as for "Little Miss Muffet". You can teach the two verses together for contrast in concept and mood or enjoy each for its own merit.

The word "grasshopper" will take on a special meaning if you shift the accent from "grass" to "hopper" — grass<u>hopper</u>. Pause after "But she said," and continue in a tough little voice. Interpret the scream as a real *scream* while drawing out the *ea* sound.

If the children or you had a particularly hard day, a couple recitations of this rhyme will help you vent some steam. But mostly, enjoy the rhyme as a comeuppance for Little Miss Tuckett.

Jeremiah Obediah

Jeremiah Obediah puffs, puffs, puffs,

When he gets his messages he snuffs, snuffs, snuffs,

When he goes to school by day he roars, roars, roars,

And when he goes to bed at night he snores, snores, snores.

Repeating the same three words in a row is not easily done. Extra diction practice will help on puffs, snuffs, roars, and snores. Selections like this are fun for children. The rhyming of "Jeremiah Obediah" will bring smiles to their faces. The beat is strong, so the delivery will have a marked rhythm.

Assign alternating lines to GIRLS and BOYS because the lines are long. Also, try mixed grouping: Group One says all the lines up to the repetitious words, and Group Two picks up the line without a break in the rhythm to say the "puffs, puffs, puffs," etc. For variety, lower the voice pitch for each "puffs" and "snuffs", then raise the voice pitch for each "roars" and "snores."

One-eyed Jack

One-eyed Jack, the pirate chief,

Was a terrible, fearsome ocean thief.

He wore a peg

Upon one leg;

He wore a hook,

And a dirty look!

One-eyed Jack, the pirate chief,

A terrible, fearsome ocean thief.

The boys might relate well to this rhyme, which sounds rough and ready. As a special treat or reward, you may choose to teach it only to the boys. Attempt low-heavy voice pitch to render this number while accenting the wonderful compilation of consonants, digraphs, and vowel sounds. The mouth will have to work hard to achieve a strong, rough-and-ready recitation.

Allocate lines in varying fashion. You might use ALL on the first two and last two lines. Group One can say the first two short lines with Group Two reciting the next couple of short lines. Without a doubt, this Mother Goose rhyme will add spice to programming.

One Misty Moisty Morning

One misty moisty morning,

    When cloudy was the weather,

I chanced to meet an old man,

    Clothed all in leather.

He began to compliment

    And I began to grin.

How do you do? And how do you do?

    And how do you do again?

There is something very special about enunciating the alliterative "misty moisty morning" with the teeth, tongue, and lips working hard to perform the line well. The story unfolds easily. The last two lines are made for fun and are my favorites. Say them expressively as if one person is saying all three lines; or, two people can greet each other. Person One says, "How do you do?" Person Two says, "And how do you do?" The last line can be a duet.

Try dividing the children into two groups. Group One recites the first two lines; Group Two the next two lines. Group One says line five; Group Two, line six. Group One asks the first "How do you do?"; Group Two responds. ALL speak line eight.

Start a silly saying around the playground or anywhere by expressively saying the three "How do you dos" to individual children, telling each one to pass them along. Let your eyes as well as your mouth do the talking. Watch what will happen in a few days.

There Was an Owl Lived in an Oak

There was an owl lived in an oak,

    Whiskey, Whaskey, Weedle;

And all the words he ever spoke

    Were Fiddle, Faddle, Feedle.

A sportsman chanced to come that way,

    Whiskey, Whaskey, Weedle;

Says he, "I'll shoot you, silly bird,

    So Fiddle, Faddle, Feedle!"

The silly owl in this rhyme falls prey to the hunter. Too much talk and no sense are uncommon traits for most owls portrayed in children's literature. The young will latch onto the "Whiskey, Whaskey, Weedle" lines readily; likewise, "Fiddle, Faddle, Feedle." The beat is steady throughout with four beats to one line and three beats to the next. Special attention is required for the voiceless *wh* on the first two words of lines two and six. Feel free to substitute the word "hunter" or "gunner" in place of "sportsman," which may connote a football, baseball, or basketball player to most children today.

Stanza one can be spoken flippantly. In stanza two, a sudden change of mood takes place when the hunter comes on the scene. Proceed cautiously and slow down the pace. On line seven voices change to a loud whisper so the owl doesn't hear the gunner and fly away. Pause after "he" in line seven and recite the remainder of the line emphatically. Enhance the last line by saying the "Fiddle, Faddle, Feedle" mockingly with appropriate facial expressions.

Group One can say verse one; Group Two, verse two. Try the rhyme in unison with a SOLO on the words, "I'll shoot you, silly bird." For a dramatic ending, ALL perform the last line.

One, Two, Buckle My Shoe

One, two, buckle my shoe.

Three, four, shut the door.

Five, six, pick up sticks.

Seven, eight, lay them straight.

Nine, ten, a big fat hen.

This number rhyme works well when recited at a fairly rapid pace with a strong four-beat-per-line count. Pithy, staccato recitation is impressive.

When children need a break from too much sitting or work, use this as an action poem by introducing simple actions to accompany the lines. My preference is to follow the jazzed-up version from the recording, "Let's All Live Together," Volume 3, by Greg Scelsa and Steve Miller. It can be found in most elementary record catalogs or in school-supply shops. A written guide accompanies the album and describes the actions. It is a crowd pleaser if you are doing a program.

For older children, you may want to recite all twenty verses. Refer to page 32 of *Tomie dePaola's Mother Goose* for the additional stanzas. Other collections include the rhyme to twenty, also.

There Was a Crooked Man

There was a crooked man,

He walked a crooked mile,

He found a crooked sixpence

Against a crooked stile;

He bought a crooked cat,

Which caught a crooked mouse,

And they all lived together

In a little crooked house.

The humor of this selection is found both in the verbal presentation of so many "crooked" things and the visual interpretation each child places on "crooked man," "crooked cat," "crooked mouse," and so forth. Hear three beats to each line. In lines seven and eight, hurry a trifle to say "And they all" and "In a little" as one beat.

Repetition of the word "crooked," plus the steady beat may cause a sing-song delivery. By means of expression and voice pitch, do whatever you can to avoid the problem. If a child asks you what a sixpence is, simply respond, "a coin worth six cents." A "stile" is a set of steps to help one climb over a wall or fence.

This Mother Goose rhyme would work well in a sequence arrangement. Use one child for each line with ALL coming in on lines seven and eight. Try other arrangements.

Pussy Cat, Pussy Cat

Pussy cat, pussy cat,

Where have you been?

I've been to London

To visit the queen.

Pussy cat, pussy cat,

What did you there?

I frightened a little mouse

Under her chair.

Use conversational speech for this dialogue selection. Every two-line sequence is a whole thought and should not be broken with a breath. Voice pitch will go up questioningly on the words "been" in line two, and "there" in line six. The cat's lines should be said proudly. Because of the length of line seven, you will have to accelerate slightly so as not to break the rhythm you have established. The *r* on "chair" will turn the children's mouths into a smile. Happily maintain that mouth position a moment or two before you stop.

Two groups or the teacher and the children may recite this poem. Two soloists would enjoy this number, also.

There Was an Old Woman

There was an old woman tossed up in a basket

Nineteen times as high as the moon;

Where was she going I couldn't but ask it,

For in her hand she carried a broom.

"Old Woman, old woman, old woman," said I,

"O whither, O whither, O whither, so high?"

"To brush the cobwebs off the sky!

And I'll be back again by and by."

This rhyme has two parts. The first stanza is mysterious, to be sure. Any child would wonder why this old lady was tossed up in a basket with her broom. An answer is given in the second part, which is a dialogue between the child and the old woman. The first two lines of the second stanza are called out by the child. Notice the pattern of three repetitions in each line. Those repetitions require clear diction and a slight pause at each comma to keep the words from running together. The old woman gives a most surprising answer in line seven and promises she will return in line eight, which brings this mystery to a satisfying conclusion for the child. Use much expression and emotion in reciting this rhyme.

Cocks Crow in the Morn

Cocks crow in the morn

To tell us to rise,

And he who lies late

Will never be wise;

For early to bed

And early to rise,

Is the way to be healthy

And wealthy and wise.

Two beats per line can be felt in this proverbial composition. Governed by the punctuation, the group can make only four pauses, the last one being a complete stop. If you use a sequential arrangement, groups could each recite either one or two lines; likewise for solos. This proverb is best performed as a unison piece because I feel unity adds more power to the meaning.

The poem may be taught with the word "one" replacing "he" in the third line. Or use "she" occasionally. The girls might like to say this poem to the boys and vice versa.

Whistle, Daughter, Whistle

Whistle, daughter, whistle,

And you shall have a sheep.

I cannot whistle, Mother,

Neither can I sleep.

Whistle, daughter, whistle,

And you shall have a cow.

I cannot whistle, Mother,

Neither know I how.

Whistle, daughter, whistle,

And you shall have a man.

I cannot whistle, Mother,

But I'll do the best I can.

The upper primary (or even older) children are entertained most with this choice. Alternate every two lines—the mother begging, the daughter complaining. Add a charming accent to this number by blowing air through puckered lips on all the voiceless *wh* sounds. Avoid slow performance or it will drag and lose some of the fun element.

Sometimes, substitute the word "Father" in place of the word "Mother." This would be appropriate for a Father's night program.

The girl whines until the last line when a sudden shift of mood takes place. Willingly and happily the daughter claims she will do her best to whistle. Immediately after the last word is said, whistle a simple tune, such as "Twinkle, Twinkle, Little Star" or "Mary Had a Little Lamb."

Most children will have trouble whistling and can identify with the daughter who does the best she can. If you can find a few fair whistlers, let them become a whistling chorus to accompany the group. Others may practice so they can join this chorus; however, do not let the children become discouraged by trying too hard.

Pease Porridge Hot

Pease porridge hot,

    Pease porridge cold,

Pease porridge in the pot,

    Nine days old.

Some like it hot,

    Some like it cold,

Some like it in the pot,

    Nine days old.

The steady beat of this rhyme makes it suitable for jump roping, skipping, or clapping. Most of the time, the playing children chant in unison. Actually, this jingle has the elements of a cheer.

"Pease Porridge Hot" would divide nicely as a sequence selection, one line for each child. Or choose a group for lines one, two, and three; ALL on line four. Another group can say lines five, six, and seven; ALL on line eight.

Spring Is Showery

Spring is showery, flowery, bowery;

Summer: hoppy, croppy, poppy;

Autumn: wheezy, sneezy, freezy;

Winter: slippy, drippy, nippy.

The unusual arrangement of the words and punctuation requires a little extra ingenuity for a pleasing rendition. The meaning of the three rhyming words in each line determine how the line is interpreted.

In the first line I sense a happy, elated feeling on "showery, flowery, bowery." A bouncy expression may serve well. "Hoppy, croppy, poppy" sounds great when done in staccato beat with a very slight pause between each word. Elongate the *ee* sound when reciting "wheezy, sneezy, freezy." If the winter lines had words like "blowy, snowy, etc.," a strong, forceful voice would be needed, but that is not the case. Short *i* in "slippy, drippy, nippy" is a delicate vowel sound. Repeat the staccato beat of line two with a slight pause between each word.

One possible arrangement for this rhyme is to have ALL say the first line, a SOLO or three SOLOS announce the seasons on the other three lines, and the whole group complete the last three lines. Or reverse the process by having ALL say the first line, ALL trumpet the season words, and nine SOLOS saying the other nine words. The SOLOS could be a mixture of effervescent and shyer children. Encourage them all to belt out their word with equal volume. Children with speech defects will relish being called on to solo a word that they are able to pronounce properly.

In a Dark, Dark Wood

In a dark, dark wood, there was a dark, dark house,

And in that dark, dark house, there was a dark, dark room,

And in that dark, dark room, there was a dark, dark cupboard,

And in that dark, dark cupboard, there was a dark, dark shelf,

And on that dark, dark shelf, there was a dark, dark box,

And in that dark, dark box, there was a GHOST!

Children respond well to the spooky rendition of this selection. Endless ways can be experimented with to achieve that mood. I do not split this poem into groups or solo lines because the children enjoy performing every line as the tension builds toward the climax.

Demonstrate how to pitch the voice deeply. Proceed slowly through the lines giving a soft emphasis to all *k*'s. It sounds extremely funny to pitch the voice up high only on the last word of each line. Drawing out the vowel digraphs *ou* in "house" and *oo* in "room" exaggerates the mood, while keeping that slow deliberate beat. The short *o* in "box" will produce the same effect.

When you near the culmination point, you may have difficulty holding the children back because the tension will be so great. After the word "box" in the last line, let them go! "There was a GHOST!" can be shouted out as they reach out their hands as if to catch someone. Audiences love to rally to the children's scare.

Another movement enjoyed by the children is the "shifty-eye movement." The children's heads and wide-open eyes move to the right on the first line and then to the left on the second line. Keep alternating throughout. Audiences will start to laugh at the children's funny facial expressions, therefore, increase the volume so the audience does not miss any words.

If All the Seas Were One Sea

If all the seas were one sea,

What a great sea that would be!

If all the trees were one tree,

What a great tree that would be!

And if all the axes were one axe,

What a great axe that would be!

And if all the men were one man,

What a great man that would be!

And if the great man took the great axe

And cut down the great tree

And let it fall into the great sea,

What a splish-splash that would be!

The first eight lines of this story poem build to the dramatic four-line culmination. The repetitious words can lead to monotony if you do not prepare well by planning the accented words.

For contrast, use SOLOS on the first four "If" lines, and ALL alternating after each SOLO. Use a moderate speed, but to create more contrast, slow down when ALL announce definitely the climactic end. "Splish-splash" terminates the excitement as the children spit out those two words. This piece is difficult to perform and should be used with upper primary or any experienced group.

Moses Supposes

Moses supposes his toeses are roses,

But Moses supposes erroneously;

For nobody's toeses are posies of roses

As Moses supposes his toeses to be.

The children get hilarious over this Mother Goose tongue twister. Begin slowly so the children will not get tongue-tied. Do not let them get frustrated initially or they will not try. The long *o* and *s* sounds are repeated throughout all four lines. A rhyme of this difficulty should not be introduced until the choral group has jelled sufficiently. Second and third graders will accept the challenge willingly. Define "erroneously" simply as "made a mistake".

Since this is such a melodius tongue twister, it should be performed in unison. Gradually increase the speed. If you get gobbledegook, practice the lines more slowly, then encourage the group to reach a moderate speed. Some will challenge themselves to a speedy recitation and succeed, perhaps surpassing the ability of the instructor.

Weather Rhymes

When clouds appear like rocks and towers,

The earth's refreshed by frequent showers.

If chickens roll in the sand,

Rain is sure to be at hand.

April weather:

Rain and sunshine, both together.

When the peacock loudly calls,

Then look out for rain and squalls.

Winter's thunder

Is the world's wonder.

Rain before seven,

Sun before eleven.

A sunshiny shower

Won't last half an hour.

March wind's and April showers,

Bring forth the May flowers.

Red sky at night

Shepherd's delight;

Red sky in the morning,

Shepherd's warning.

(The word "Sailor" may be substituted for the word "Shepherd.")

These traditional weather rhymes, some familiar and some unfamiliar, should be in every child's repertoire and can be taught during appropriate seasons or weather conditions. As the weather prompts, the appropriate ditty may be spoken at any time of the day. Before long the children might check out the weather and invite you and the group to join a rhyme.

Encourage the children to observe sunrise or sunset, then, with a short explanation, the "Red sky" verse will have meaning for them.

The maxims are short. Therefore, more ingenuity is required to convey their messages well. Let the words and the moods of each ditty be your guide to interpretation. One caution: avoid sing-song recitation of these short verses.

Step Jingles

Step in a hole,

You'll break your mother's bowl.

Step on a crack,

You'll break your mother's back.

Step in a ditch,

Your mother's nose will itch.

Step in the dirt,

You'll tear your father's shirt.

Step on a nail,

You'll put your father in jail.

I came across this set of five step jingles when I did research for this book. The second jingle brings back memories of my childhood in Detroit when my little friends and I chanted the following as we walked a mile to and from school:

Step on a line
You break your mother's spine.
Step on a crack
You break your mother's back.

Although we zigzagged our steps to school, we never came late and even had time to stop at the candy shop if we had extra pennies.

You can present these couplets, and the version I learned as a child, as one whole selection or as two-liners. Walking, jump roping, and skipping are perfect movements for these jingles.

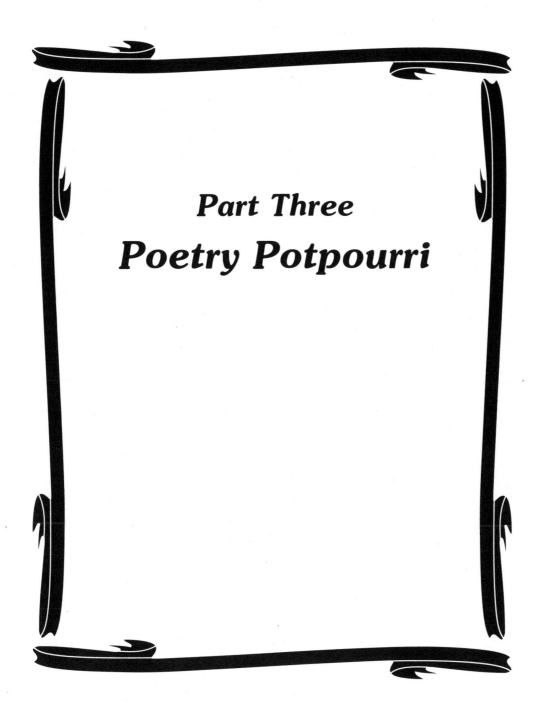

Part Three
Poetry Potpourri

Timbuctoo

In Timbuctoo,

In Timbuctoo.

There are the nicest things to do:

The monkeys play in the cocoanut trees,

And the shore slopes down to the purple seas,

And a pirate's treasure is on the beach,

And little brown ponies are just in reach;

And there aren't any clocks,

And there aren't any bells,

And what the time is, nobody tells—

For everyone does what he wants to do,

In Timbuctoo,

In Timbuctoo.

Marchette Chute

Once they say this poem, kids want to visit Timbuctoo often. The long lines of Chute's poem adapt beautifully to sequence recitation. To give the vocalization a strong start and finish, ask ALL to say the first and last three lines. The overall mood is happiness, but capture the mood of each line. There is an automatic slowdown on the "clocks," "bells," and "time" lines. Give all the children a chance to SOLO. You can also test out other arrangements for large or small groups.

The Moon's the North Wind's Cooky
(What the Little Girl Said)

The Moon's the North Wind's cooky.

He bites it, day by day,

Until there's but a rim of scraps

That crumble all away.

The South Wind is a baker.

He kneads clouds in his den,

And bakes a crisp new moon that ... greedy

North ... Wind ... eats ... again!

Vachel Lindsay

This selection is one of Vachel Lindsay's most famous, oft-quoted compositions for children. He is one of the greatest traveling troubadours of poetry in our recent past. You might claim him as your model and share a rhyme wherever you go.

The children need to identify with the rich imagery of the three main characters—the Moon, the North Wind, and the South Wind. They should also understand what part each character plays in this little poetic drama. The punctuation is well marked for easy performance. The word "knead" should be defined.

Perform in an expressive storytelling voice. GIRLS and BOYS can alternate verses or lines; or experiment with four mixed groups reciting two lines each.

Follow up study of the moon or a story about the moon, with this creative composition. As a bonus, the children will learn the difference between fact and fiction.

The Admiration of Willie

Grown folks are wise

About tying ties

And baking cakes

And chasing aches,

Building walls

And finding balls

And making planes

And cars and trains—

And kissing children into bed

After their prayers are said.

Gwendolyn Brooks

Youngsters choose many heroes to pattern their lives after. Willie's admiration of grown-ups is wonderful for the children to share. Everyday happenings, ordinary and extraordinary, are packed into this rhyme. The setup of lines adapts well to sequence vocalization—one line per child. However, the first line and the two closing lines would add impact to the performance if ALL said them.

If entertaining adults at any program, this selection will exalt their accomplishments. The children, too, receive satisfaction in singing the praises of their grown-up heroes. After all, they will someday be on the receiving end of Willie's admiration.

Too Sad

It's such a shock, I almost screech,

When I find a worm inside my peach!

But then, what *really* makes me blue

Is to find a worm who's bit in two!

William Cole

"Too Sad" deserves a dramatic recitation. A few directors may be squeamish about "that half-eaten worm" but the children disgustingly relish that phrase as evident in their facial maneuverings. Take your time in saying this poem and give full pauses at the punctuation. A full breath will be needed to go from "what" in line three to the end.

In unity there is power and this should be a unison recitation. However, you could direct GIRLS on lines one and two; BOYS on lines three and four, or vice versa. Enjoy this peach of a poem!

Up a Tree

The branch of a tree

Is perfect for me

It's the best place that I've ever found.

I'm sure, if I could,

I would stay here for good,

And never return to the ground.

William Wise

A monologue rhyme, "Up a Tree" will be a favorite for outdoor-type kids and those who wish they could be. The rhythm and context call for a moderate-slow recitation. The rhyme is well metered and you can hear two beats in lines one and two, and three beats in the third line of each verse. Because of the length of the third line, hustle to fit in the words easily using good articulation. The last line has one less syllable so you will not have any problem there.

Try any two groupings, one for each verse. If you do a program, this composition would be an ideal SOLO for a rough and sturdy child with a booming voice. The child tells the story with fists placed at the waist on each side and feet spread apart slightly. The smaller the child (K-1), the funnier the rendition. Prepare the child for the audience's obvious reaction and have him or her respond with a big smile and a bow.

The Baby Goes to Boston

What does the train say?
    Jiggle joggle, jiggle joggle!
What does the train say?
    Jiggle joggle jee!
Will the little baby go
Riding with the locomo?
Loky moky poky stoky
    Smoky choky chee!

Ting! ting! the bells ring,
    Jiggle joggle, jiggle joggle!
Ting! ting! the bells ring,
    Jiggle joggle jee!
Ring for joy because we go
Riding with the locomo,
Loky moky poky stoky
    Smoky choky chee!

Look! how the trees run,
    Jiggle joggle, jiggle joggle!
Each chasing t' other one,
    Jiggle joggle jee!
Are they running for to go
Riding with the locomo?
Loky moky poky stoky
    Smoky choky chee!

Over the hills now,
    Jiggle joggle, jiggle joggle!
Down through the vale below,
    Jiggle joggle jee!
All the cows and horses run,
Crying, "Won't you take us on,
Loky moky poky stoky
    Smoky choky chee?"

So, so, the miles go,
  Jiggle joggle, jiggle joggle!
Now it's fast and now it's slow,
  Jiggle joggle jee!
When we're at our journey's end,
Say good-by to snorting friend,
Loky moky poky stoky
  Smoky choky chee!

Laura E. Richards

The refrain poem, "The Baby Goes to Boston," is not as hard to teach as it looks. The children need to learn only the four refrain lines. The director reads or recites the whole narrative. Teach this story rhyme after the second semester of first grade. By then, they have a good hold on consonants, consonant blends, and digraphs, which are plentiful in these refrain lines.

Write the two "Jiggle joggle" lines on a chalkboard so the children can see they are different. Number them 1 and 2. Write "Loky moky" etc. in columnar form so the children can visualize the *oky* rhyming element. Number this column 3. You could letter these lines on a large chart for future use.

Practice the lines slowly at first, hitting all the *j* and *g* sounds. Get that wheel motion into the words by going faster and faster. The "oky" rhyming words will be as tricky as a tongue twister to learn, but the youngsters love the sounds. Start slowly. Increase the speed to equal that of the other refrain lines. When fairly mastered, attempt reciting the selection together.

Begin by tugging twice on an imaginary rope while blasting the train whistle, "Woooo-woooo!" and start full speed ahead. With the rhythm rumble of the wheels in your voice, ask, "What does the train say?" Use a pointer to point to line 1. The children recite keeping the beat. Say the next line and point to 2 for the children to pick it up. Recite the next two lines and point to 3 so the children say the column of rhyming words with the "chee" at the end. Proceed through all five verses in this manner.

The words of verse five call for a slowdown in speed. After the last word, the whole group again tugs twice with one hand on the train whistle and lets out a mournful "Woooo-woooooo-oooooo," trailing loud to soft. Use an arching and off-to-the-right arm movement. With a dip of your hand, the whistle stops. The children quickly grab onto these refrain lines. Do not overpractice. After several weeks the results will be fantastic.

The Big Clock

Slowly ticks the big clock;

Tick-tock, tick-tock!

But cuckoo clock ticks double quick;

Tick-a-tock-a, tick-a-tock-a,

Tick-a-tock-a, tick!

Unknown

This experience poem may not be within the experience of some children because electric and digital clocks sit silently in their homes. Introduce the poem by demonstrating a windup clock and a cuckoo clock, if you have those. However, a verbal explanation will suffice.

The voice imitates the rhythm of a clock (or metronome) as the lines are said. Say lines one and two in a natural low tone. Quicken the pace and lighten the tone as lines three, four, and five are delivered. When the *ck* sounds are pronounced separately, you will achieve the clock-ticking sound, e.g., *ti ck, to ck*. You may want to teach this rhyme when presenting the *ck* sound in phonics.

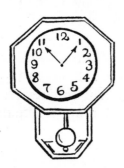

Things to Do If You Are a Subway

Pretend you are a dragon.

Live in underground caves.

Roar about underneath the city.

Swallow piles of people.

Spit them out at the next station.

Zoom through the darkness.

Go fast.

Make as much noise as you please.

Bobbi Katz

Children who have ridden on subway trains will identify with the imagery in Katz's city poem. Others will profit by a discussion of subways to bring the images to light. The ideas and well-constructed words make this number dynamic.

What could be more fun than playing subway dragon in choral speaking? Pretending is grossly underdeveloped in many children today because of too much television, videos, and toys. The imagery in this poem will motivate children to use their imaginations.

Initial action verbs propel each line to its finish. Use voices to capacity on "roar," "swallow," "spit," and "zoom." You have no specific rhythm to follow, so capitalize on diction and expression. Actually "roar" and swallow "piles of people." The alliteration on the popping *p* sounds helps pop the people into the dragon's subway door mouth. Spit out every *t* in line five. Stretch the *z* and *oo* on "zoom." Be dragons having a rip-roaring time!

The layout of lines is perfect for sequence reciting. But the overall mood generates power, so you could recite this selection in unison or with two large groups.

All Dressed Up

He wore three pair of glasses

And an apple on his head.

His shoes were fine banana skin,

His nose was cherry red.

His coat was made of poppy seeds,

His cane hung from his ear,

And when he caught a bumble-bee,

He calmly flew away.

Arnold Spilka

Spilka's nonsense rhymes are funny bone ticklers for kids. Recite this rhyme slowly so the children have time to form their own imagery. Put exaggerated expression into all adjectives and nouns as you herald this ridiculous "all dressed up" fellow.

Use facial expressions of wonderment and doubt. The eyes can be used for effect in this number. Start line one with no widening of the eyes. On each succeeding line, widen the eyes slightly while increasing the volume gradually. By the time you reach the climatic scarey word, "bumble-bee," the eyes should be stretched wide open, the volume loud. I believe most children and adults have a natural fear of this creature.

An abrupt change in mood occurs on the last line, which should be reflected in the speaking chorus. The word "calmly" breaks the tension. Let the words of line eight flit out to bring this nonsensical ditty to a fitting end.

Two mixed groups or BOYS and GIRLS could recite two lines each with ALL building up the last two culmination lines. Seven SOLOS could also perform one line each. Arrange the SOLOS so their voice pitches can build the crescendo. ALL seven recite the last line.

Sleep, Baby, Sleep

Sleep, baby, sleep!

Thy father watches the sheep.

Thy mother is shaking the dreamland tree,

And down falls a little dream for thee.

Sleep, baby, sleep!

Sleep, baby, sleep!

The large stars are the sheep.

The little stars are the lambs, I guess.

The bright moon is the shepherdess.

Sleep, baby, sleep!

Old German Lullaby

The words of this lullaby call for a dreamy rendition. When speaking quietly, give extra attention to enunciation and voice projection. Observe the commas and recite the following line in soft modulation.

Slee p, ba by, slee p!

Build up lines two and three to a medium crescendo until the word "tree." The pace should accelerate. In line four, the words, "down falls," require a contrasting diminuendo to the word "thee." Slow down the pace.

Try a slight pause between the two verses so that the repetitious "sleep" lines do not run together. Repeat the crescendo-decrescendo pattern established in the first stanza. The figurative language may necessitate a short explanation or discussion. If you use the words "let's pretend," the children will have no trouble understanding dreamland tree, little stars as lambs, and the moon as a lady shepherd. The beauty and imagery of this piece would be ruined if even the slightest body movement was introduced.

The Frog on the Log

There once

Was a green

Little frog, frog, frog—

Who played

In the wood

On a log, log, log!

A screech owl

Sitting

In a tree, tree, tree—

Came after

The frog

With a scree, scree, scree!

When the frog

Heard the owl—

In a flash, flash, flash—

He leaped

In the pond

With a splash, splash, splash!

Ilo Orleans

This frequently anthologized composition by Ilo Orleans is a real winner for choral speakers. Playfully recite the first two verses. Make an abrupt change of pace on the third verse as you say the words with caution in your voice. Pick up speed on verse four and increase it steadily until that frog is down under water with the last "splash"!

The rhythm in this number is very strong and should be maintained throughout. The repetitious words could be spoken in even rhythm, or you could attempt a jazzier beat by saying the first two "frog" words quickly, frog, frog *(pause)* frog. It is not easy to say the "frog" words in rhythm and hear all the ending *g* sounds, but try. The *ee* in "tree" and "scree" force the children's mouths into a wide toothy grin. Also, the *sh* digraph in the end position on "flash" and "splash" require attention.

The rhythm, the words, and the rhyme of this piece are so much fun that introducing actions would be superfluous except at the last "splash." If you use the "splash" action, model for the children just when they should put their fingertips together at waist height, raise the hands quickly and throw the arms up in perfect time with the last word. Exaggerate that last *sh* loudly by holding onto it while keeping the arms fully extended. Motion for the cutoff. All sound stops! Arms come gently down to the sides.

Various groupings can be tried.

Snail's Pace

Maybe it's so

that snails are slow.

They trudge along and tarry.

But isn't it true

you'd slow up, too,

If you had a house to carry?

Aileen Fisher

Matter-of-fact expression and a slow, deliberate recitation are suitable for this humorous snail poem. A slight pause after "slow," "tarry," and "too," add a complementary touch to this selection. You can establish a working rhythm if you tap two beats in the first two lines and three beats in the last line of each verse.

The second part builds up to a pointed climax with a questioning expression throughout. When reciting this verse, your voice tends to get louder with each line, but never exceed a moderate volume at any point.

After unison work and one-group-a-verse practice, test out sequence arrangements. Three groups can each recite one sentence. You, the GIRLS, and the BOYS can each take one sentence. Or three SOLO children can recite a sentence. This could be a charming SOLO number for use in a performance.

Way Down South

Way down South where the bananas grow,

A grasshopper stepped on an elephant's toe.

The elephant said, with tears in his eyes,

"Can't you pick on somebody your own little size?"

Anonymous

The children revel at the incongruity of this selection. Spoken in unison and with gusto to a strong beat, it makes for a rousing rendition. The last line has more syllables and the children need diction practice to say the words quickly, concisely, and not break the beat. Otherwise, the punch line is lost.

Have the children raise their voices to a high falsetto on the quote. They enjoy that as their faces pout to perfection. Even a large group can achieve a soft, whining, feeling-sorry-for-myself expression.

Occasionally, try a few solos on the last line. This gives the children a chance to be entertained by each other. When the group starts "going bananas," you have gone one SOLO too many.

Keeper of the Sheep

My sheep hear my voice

and come to me.

      I am a keeper of the sheep.

I call my sheep by name

and lead them out to pasture.

      I am a keeper of the sheep.

I walk ahead of them

and they follow me.

      I am a keeper of the sheep.

If a wolf attacks the flock,

I will protect them.

      I am a keeper of the sheep.

When a little lamb strays,

I will go after it and carry it home.

      I am a keeper of the sheep.

I count all my sheep at the gate.

Not one shall be lost.

      I am a keeper of the sheep.

          Rose Marie Anthony

My adaptation of the story of "The Good Shepherd" is written in antiphonal style. It is poetic prose, having neither a determined meter nor rhyme, although it is shaped in a couplet form. Recite slowly and prayerfully. The antiphon necessitates as least two groups — one performing the story line, the other, the antiphon. More groups are suitable as well as SOLO lines after the children are comfortable with the recitation. Even the antiphon could be spoken by a confident SOLO.

Avoid any stops in the couplet lines until you reach a comma or a period. The vocabulary is very simple. To render this selection in an overdramatic way will spoil the mood.

Get 'Em Here

"Hot dogs with sauerkraut

Cold drinks, here!

Hot dogs with sauerkraut

Get 'em here!

Hot dogs with sauerkraut

Cold drinks here!"

Shouts the man as he rolls the city's smallest store

All tucked neatly under a huge, blue and

orange striped umbrella.

Lee Bennett Hopkins

To understand this city rhyme, some children may need an explanation of a street vendor. Perhaps a picture or a chalkboard drawing will help. Some may have memories of seeing one at a town parade, the beach, in a ball park stadium, or at the circus.

Teach the children to pitch their voices lower to imitate the street vendor's cry when belting out his menu. Pay particular attention to the many *d* and *t* words.

It might be fun to divide the boys into two groups with BOYS 1 calling out the first two lines, BOYS 2 the next two lines, and ALL BOYS on lines five and six. GIRLS can pick it up at the word "Shouts" and communicate the description of the little store on wheels. With the younger ones, sneak a breath after the word "store." Third grade lung capacity will probably get the group through the three closing lines without a break. Individuals may catch a breath along the way and not be heard. Switch GIRLS to the vendor's lines. Experiment with SOLO or mixed groupings, too.

Yellow

Yellow lemon

Yellow hand bell

Yellow clothing

Yellow stair well

Yellow giraffe

Yellow brick road

Yellow pencil

Yellow seed sowed

Yellow crayon

Yellow song bird

Yellow flower

Yellow cheese curd

Mary Ellen Paulson

Children have a super fun time with this rhyme even though it is challenging. With twelve repetitions of the word "Yellow" in the initial position of the lines, the problem is to avoid monotonous recitation. Clipping along at a moderate pace helps to avoid monotony. Clear, crisp pronunciations and poignant word projection are needed to capture this rich array of consonants.

After the words are learned, a sequence performance could be very effective—one line per child. Individual voice pitches and expression will add color, including yellow, to the verbalization.

With a class of twenty-four, try two children a line. If your class number is odd, put three in the last group or you fill in to make the last group of two. Keep the children alert so that they are able to comfortably come in on their line without breaking the beat. If you overmotivate, they might tense and say their line prematurely.

At early primary levels, take advantage of this rhyme when teaching the *l* sound in three positions in the word or the initial *y* sound.

A few phrases may require an explanation. Refer to "The Wizard of Oz" when explaining the "yellow brick road." Most city kids will need "sowed" and "cheese curd" defined. A true Wisconsinite, Paulson squeezed that cheese curd in before her rhyme terminated!

The Light-hearted Fairy

Oh, who is so merry, so merry, heigh ho!

As the light-hearted fairy? heigh ho!

Heigh ho!

He dances and sings

To the sound of his wings,

With a hey and a heigh and a ho!

Oh, who is so merry, so airy, heigh ho!

As the light-hearted fairy? heigh ho!

Heigh ho!

His nectar he sips

From the primroses lips,

With a hey and a heigh and a ho!

Oh, who is so merry, so merry, heigh ho!

As the light-hearted fairy? Heigh ho!

Heigh ho!

The night is his noon

And the sun is the moon,

With a hey and a heigh and a ho!

Anonymous

Trip along lightly at a fast pace when reciting this poem. Because of the speed and strong beat of the composition, the teeth, tongue, and lips work hard. Executed energetically, these verses can tire the children, not to mention the director. Perhaps learning one stanza a day, after you have introduced the whole piece, would be suitable. The *h* sounds are many and demand much breath, causing the children to peter out. Motivate highly before starting.

The repeated "heigh hos" propel this rhyme right to the end. Pronounce "heigh" with a long *i* sound. "Hey" already has the long *a* sound. The fourth and fifth lines of the last two stanzas may require some clarification.

Once memorized, you may give the children a rest at midrecitation by speaking the fourth and fifth lines of each stanza or choose SOLOS to do so. That electrifying power I spoke of in part 1 is felt deeply if the chorus delivers this composition enthusiastically.

After a Bath

After my bath

I try, try, try

to wipe myself

till I'm dry, dry, dry.

Hands to wipe

and fingers and toes

and two wet legs

and a shiny nose.

Just think how much

less time I'd take

if I were a dog

and could shake, shake, shake.

Aileen Fisher

This humorous experience poem has sparse end punctuation, so catch a breath at the end of every two lines. Pausing before the periods will break the rhythm. Because of the varying number of syllables in each line, it is easy to hear three beats per line. Some words automatically run together on one beat.

<u>After</u> my bath

<u>I try</u>, try, try

<u>to wipe</u> myself

<u>till</u> I'm dry, dry, dry.

Concentrate hard on diction as the combination of consonants, blends, and digraphs demand strenuous teeth, tongue and lip work. Actions throughout this poem would detract from the delightful words. However, to accompany the climax, you might simply shake arms and hands in three, quick, downward movements on each "shake."

Family Tree
(An Unsuccessful Falling Out)

Ma Tree

is in a quandary.

"It's fall—it's time to go!" she says

and gives her children's heads

a little shake to make

her point. But leaves mistake

the green below

and cry, "No, no,

it's spring!"

and cling.

Irene Zimmerman

The imagery of the selection presents both amusement and puzzlement. Thinking of the leaves as Ma Tree's kids amuses all. Utter the first sentence as announcing a dilemma. Firmly, Ma Tree gives the command. A full breath after "she says" helps the group to say the next line through to the period.

The leaf children lack the wisdom and experience of Mother Tree and rebel at the thought of falling to the ground just yet. Complainingly, they talk back. A slight break after the word "spring" will supply added weight to the last line which can be spoken most emphatically. Use this selection with experienced choral groups.

Funny Bunny

Bunny ears!

Bunny ears!

Wiggle, wiggle, wiggle!

Funny ears!

Funny ears!

Jiggle, jiggle, jiggle!

Run and hop!

Run and hop!

Do not stop!

Do not stop!

FUNNY BUNNY!

Rose Marie Anthony

"Funny Bunny" is a wiggle-time rhyme for young children. It is a whole-body action poem but you can adapt it for a fingerplay.

To start, tell the children to find a little piece of space for themselves. Begin in a stand-up-straight position, hands at the sides. The exclamation points indicate emphatic delivery on every line. The first two lines are spoken and, for the third line, the children place one hand on each side of the top of their heads. All five fingers should be straight up and close together like bunny ears with the palms facing forward. Bend the fingers forward once for each "wiggle." Hands drop immediately to the sides. Repeat this action sequence for the next three lines.

For the four "run, hop, stop" lines, the children take a step-and-a-hop on each line, almost like a skip but not as fast. Remind them to have their inner radar tuned on so they do not bump into anyone. After the last "stop," the youngsters should stand still. Show them how to hold one hand on each side of the waist and, in rhythm, nod the head once on each word of the last line. As you say, "FUNNY BUNNY," hold onto the *n* sound a bit. Should you use this poem as a choral selection without the actions, try some grouping.

Andre

I had a dream last night. I dreamed

I had to pick a Mother out.

I had to choose a Father, too.

At first, I wondered what to do,

There were so many there, it seemed,

Short and tall and thin and stout.

But just before I sprang awake,

I knew what parents I would take.

And this surprised and made me glad:

They were the ones I always had!

Gwendolyn Brooks

This dream delight pleases children and equally so, their parents. The word content implies dreamy, wondering expression for voicing this selection. In lines five and six, vocalize dilemma and amazement at being presented with so many choices. In line six, draw out the variety words and diminish all the "ands," like so:

<u>Short</u> and <u>tall</u> and <u>thin</u> and <u>stout</u>.

The mood changes and the pace quickens after line six. Try building a moderate crescendo through to the last word. Punctuation pops up midline sometimes. To interpret the meaning smoothly, stop or pause only at the punctuation marks. In any program where mothers and fathers are present, this composition is sure to be a parent pleaser.

I Thank You, God

I THANK you, God,

For a hundred things;

For the flower that blooms,

For the bird that sings,

For the sun that shines,

For the rain that drops,

For *ice cream*,

And *raisins*,

And *lollipops*.

Amen!

Ilo Orleans

Ilo Orleans' happy thank-you poem written for his daughter and son long ago is as contemporary today as it was then. Do not teach this rhyme with a soft, prayerful expression, but rather, use a vibrant, jubilant manner to accent the many happy everyday images. Yes! It is a joyful song of thanks.

Emphasize the words "THANK" and "hundred" by lifting the voice pitch. Lines three and four can be delivered joyously but tenderly. For contrast, recite lines five and six with a feel of sun and rain coming down. The three short lines can be said more slowly and deliciously while savoring the words. This "Amen" may sound irreverent to some, but it comes out a loud "A-----------men"!

A sequence arrangement with groups or SOLOS on lines one through six is suitable. ALL say the last four lines. The reverse is equally effective with ALL chiming in on "Amen!"

Dusting

Come! Rearrange the dust!

Use broom and mop just so!

When dust is heaped in little piles,

It's neater, don't you know.

Emily Oszewski

Most children have had the experience of helping their parents sweep or watching a maintenance person push a broom. This earthy poem gently sings the praises of cleaning up.

The words suggest a moderate-slow pace. Exclamation points indicate a matter-of-fact recitation. Pronounced pauses are fitting at the commas in lines three and four.

In classrooms or homes, children should be given the opportunity to "rearrange the dust" for real and for play. "Dusting" could be a charming SOLO for a program.

Voice of the Sky

The sky has the oldest voice

that ever has been heard—

it sighs,

it roars,

it cries,

yet never speaks a word.

Over the hill it comes

through treetops autumn-thinned—

it sings,

it moans,

it hums.

Listen, the wind, the wind!

Aileen Fisher

"Voice of the Sky" is for children well versed in choral speaking, be they first, second, or third graders (or older). The rhyme pattern is more sophisticated, with only the second and sixth lines rhyming. Following the punctuation, the first and second lines are spoken with no break. "Through treetops autumn-thinned" may require extra diction practice and perhaps a simple explanation of the imagery.

The short lines beginning with "it" contain six verbs, all of which call for contrasting vocal interpretation. Use a lilting voice on "sighs" and "sings." The long *o* sound in "moans" and "roars" calls for a deeper voice and a raise in volume while slightly prolonging the *o* sound. "Cries" is mournful; "hums" is happy.

But the last line is the powerful summation to this whole composition and leaves the final impact. Pause at both commas. Start out softly on "Listen" and build the volume upward to "wind." The three *n* sounds can be held slightly so the hum of the wind can be clearly heard. Pronounce the *d* softly on each "wind."

Besides unison recitation, a sequential line arrangement for small groups could be effective with ALL saying the last line of each verse. For programming, this title could make a powerful SOLO for a full voice.

Popcorn

Dance, little corn seeds,

Hop, hop, hop!

Soon we shall hear you

Pop, pop, pop!

Keep on dancing

Please do not stop

Till our pan is full

To the TOP, TOP, TOP!

Anonymous

"Popcorn" is one of the oldest poems in my repertoire. I have taught this rhyme to many hundreds of children over the years. Some children will convert "hop" to "pop" in line two. If you write the two lines on the chalkboard the children will see the difference and remember.

Lively, crisp rendition of these words is effective. A staccato beat on the hop, top, and pop lines works well. Keep the pace rapid. On the last "TOP" ALL pronounce the voiceless *p* in perfect unison. Teach this number in unison—breaking it up makes it lose power and volume. Try groupings if you like.

Some words call for noise during delivery. Ask the children to clap once on each "hop," "pop," and "TOP"—nine claps. As they pronounce the voiceless *p* on the last "TOP," they throw up their hands as high as they can reach. The clapping builds up the momentum and heightens the excitement.

Something about Me

There's something about me

That I'm knowing.

There's something about me

That isn't showing.

I'm growing!

Anonymous

This simple five-liner is undoubtedly within the experience of every child. You might want to teach it to every small child you meet.

Articulate the first four lines in a charming and winsome way. The children's facial expressions will either make or break this poem. Add the following significant gesture, if you like. As the children say sentence one, they raise their right hands slightly with the "pointer" finger extended in the "pay attention" manner. At the beginning of the second sentence, do the same with the left hand. (Right hands will be back at their sides.)

The crowning point is the last two words. Smile! Proudly and definitively announce "I'm growing!" as the whole group moves up onto tippy-toes in unison. This last movement takes practice. Ask the children to separate their feet a little to prevent hobble and bobble. If you are on carpeting, it is more of a challenge.

Hippopotamusses

Hippopotamusses never

Put on boots in rainy weather.

To slosh in mud up to their ears

Brings them great joy and merry tears.

Their pleasure lies in being messed up

They just won't play at being dressed up.

In fact a swamp is heaven plus

If you're a hippopotamus.

Arnold Spilka

Surprise the children by printing or writing this title in large letters across a chalkboard or long roll of paper. Children respond with laughter at this very long, silly-looking word. Saying it is even more fun.

Present the rhyme on any day or use it as a follow-up to a unit on zoo or jungle animals. It can also be used with some of the wonderful picture books about hippos. The images of this poem are clear, but a child may ask the meaning of "merry tears."

Avoid pauses where there is no end punctuation, except after the words "messed up." That line is a complete thought. Because of the length of the double lines, this is clearly not a selection for early beginners in choral speaking. Two groups can nicely relate two lines in alternating fashion. Unison voicing is also fun.

The Squirrel

Whisky, frisky,

Hippity hop,

Up he goes

To the tree top!

Whirly, twirly,

Round and round,

Down he scampers

To the ground.

Furly, curly,

What a tail!

Tall as a feather

Broad as a sail!

Where's his supper?

In the shell,

Snappity, crackity,

Out it fell.

Unknown

"The Squirrel" is a poem included in most comprehensive anthologies, and rightly so. Children who experience squirrels in and around their neighborhood identify whole-heartedly with this bushy-tailed friend; others may wish they had squirrels for neighbors.

A squirrel moves quickly about, running, scampering here and there. These four verses, likewise, can be vocalized at a running pace for dynamic effect. "Up" in verse one indicates crescendo; "down" in verse two calls for a winddown but only to a moderate volume.

Make that tail very impressive in verse three by observing the exclamation point! Teach the children to raise their voice pitch, from low to high, quickly on the word "tall," and to stretch the vowel sound in "broad" without destroying the rhythm.

Verse four leads with a question, indicating a rising inflection on "supper." The answer follows matter-of-factly. Two claps of the hands on "snappity, crackity" is emphatic and complements the imagery.

Taking Off

The airplane taxis down the field

And heads into the breeze,

It lifts its wheels above the ground,

It skims above the trees,

It rises high and higher

Away up toward the sun,

It's just a speck against the sky

—And now it's gone!

Unknown

The observer on the ground can feel the takeoff and ascension of the plane through the sequence of lines in this selection. Very simply, direct this poem with a crescendo building from line one to line seven. The dash marks a prominent pause at the beginning of line eight. An abrupt drop in volume, speed, and mood overtakes the group. Each word in line eight receives equal emphasis. Voices and faces should register disappointment at the disappearance of the plane.

This rhyme works in a sequence arrangement—one line per child. Seven SOLOS could take a line with ALL coming in on the last line; however, it may be difficult to pick the voices that can build the upward crescendo. Test out other arrangements, too.

Teeth

Brush your teeth;

Floss each day.

Lovely smile;

Less decay.

Mary Ellen Paulson

This health rhyme can long be remembered and passed on from generation to generation, because of its simplicity.

What can be more beautiful than a child's smile? Obviously this selection is appropriate to introduce or follow up a dental lesson or program. The words "floss" and "decay" can be explained in the health presentation.

Do a vim-and-vigor interpretation of this piece. The children can all sound like teachers. They love imitating teachers as you well know. Ask all to break into a "Lovely smile"; then, in contrast, express straight faces with chins dropped to say, "Less decay."

You can be sure this health rhyme will be taught to the whole family. It might prompt each child to practice privately in front of the mirror every time the teeth are brushed and flossed.

Pussy Willow Song

I know a little pussy,

Her coat is silver gray,

She lives down in the meadow,

Not so very far away.

Although she is a pussy,

She'll never be a cat,

For she's a pussy willow—

Now, what do you think of that?

Meow, meow, meow, meow,

Meow, meow, meow, meow, SCAT!!!

American Folk Song

This rhyme is a song, a charming choral speaking piece, and a fun-time activity number.

The lines fit well into a sequence arrangement—one line per child. ALL can chime in on the "meows" and "SCAT." Or if you choose unison or couplets on the first eight lines, try SOLO voices, one on each "meow," with no break in the rhythm. Use experienced groups since this will take much practice to make the eight "meows" flow smoothly. ALL shout "SCAT"!

Use this rhyme for exercise or playtime. Start by having the children squat, feet flat on the floor. On each line starting from line two, raise the body just a little. By line eight the children should be standing tall. Then start the descent on each "meow." You should be back in the squatting position by the eighth "meow." Jump high on SCAT!

News Story

When Peter Lumpkin was a youth,

Imagine this! He lost a tooth!

When interviewed by a reporter

He said, "You know, I found a quarter

Beneath my pillow—without doubt

I ought to knock the others out.

I know I may look kind of funny,

But goodness! I'll get lots of money!"

William Cole

Losing a tooth is a front page "news story" in every primary-grade child's life.

There is a lot of midline punctuation in this selection to help in reciting. Take no pauses after "reporter," "quarter," and "doubt." Register voices in exclamation at the four exclamation points. "Without doubt I should knock the others out," should take on a brave tone, almost bragging. Follow with contrasting sheepishness: "I know I may look kind of funny." You might have the children cover their mouths loosely to sustain the volume. Try stretching "good" on "goodness." Equally emphasizing "lots" and "money" will bring this number to a satisfying end.

GIRLS can begin with the first four lines through "He said." BOYS can herald the remaining lines between the quotations marks. This selection can also be tried with some SOLO lines.

The Frog

What a wonderful bird the frog are—

When he stand he sit almost;

When he hop, he fly almost.

He ain't got no sense hardly;

He ain't got no tail hardly either.

When he sit, he sit on what he ain't got almost.

Anonymous

Since children are taught they "ain't" supposed to say "ain't," they love this piece of poetry. The nonsensical content and the unusual placement of words in the lines turn this selection into a funny bone tickler. It is fun to say in unison recitation. However, it is suitable for grouping if you so choose.

Speak each line slowly and expressively so every ridiculous thought can be savored and pictured mentally. Crescendo slightly from line one through line five. Diminish the volume for line six. Make a definite pause after the first "sit" and the word "got." For special effect, pronounce the "almost" together, saying each syllable most emphatically. This rhyme is a certain winner for programs.

Mud

Mud is very nice to feel

All squishy-squash between the toes!

I'd rather wade in wiggly mud

Than smell a yellow rose.

Nobody else but the rosebush knows

How nice mud feels

Between the toes.

Polly Chase Boyden

Mud and children attract each other. To execute this number satisfactorily, pause only at the three punctuation marks. Accent every other syllable to get a rhythm going. In the fifth line you have to squeeze in a few extra syllables.

Deliver the first verse in moderate-low tones to accent the mood shift in the second part. Pitch voices high on "Nobody else but the" and drop lower on "rosebush knows." The words "nice," "feels," "between," and "toes," can be oozed out slowly to exemplify mud. Notice how the lips pucker up and the noses wrinkle as the children pronounce that wonderful *squ* sound. The fourth line has two *ell* words which add texture—smell and yellow.

The figurative language in the last three lines may need explaining, but usually some child will know that the rosebush's toes are her roots. Because of the playful impact this poem has on the children, use it mostly as a unison number.

Simone (My Cat)

We share a chair,

Simone and I.

She leaves her hair

To mark the place

Where she has lain

And makes it plain

That, though we share

That single chair,

She holds the claim.

Emily Oszewski

Animals are creatures of habit as Emily Oszewski's cat experience explains. Children who have pets understand the cat's claim on the shared chair. But those without pets may need briefing. Just as children or grown-ups place a newspaper, toy, book, or other object on a chair to save it until their momentary return, the cat sheds her hair on the chair as her "mine" mark.

Do not hurry when reciting this poem. Pause at all the punctuation marks and after the word "lain," or the breath supply may run out. Very definitively speak every word in the last line with Simonic authority.

Try this selection as a SOLO performance for program use. Expressive unison recitation can be enjoyable. Another possibility is ALL on lines one and two, Group One on the next three lines, Group Two on lines six, seven, and eight, and ALL on the final line.

Peanut Butter Cheer

Peanut, peanut, peanut butter!

Peanut, peanut, peanut butter!

Spread it on your bread;

Do it like I said!

Peanut, peanut, peanut butter!

Peanut, peanut, peanut butter!

and JELLY!

Rose Marie Anthony

Space is needed for movement on this rousing activity rhyme. Use the aisles between the desks, the playground, wherever. The directions sound complicated but are very simple when combined with the words. Master the movements and words before working with the children. You may wish to design your own actions to accompany this rhyme.

The children loosely line up in rows, shoulder to shoulder, and face you. You model the movements starting slowly. On every "peanut" in the first line, do a sideways step-close movement to the right. (When you get moving, your step becomes a mini-hop.) Simultaneously, with both hands down, side by side, and moving to the right, open the fingers on "pea-" and close them on "-nut" three times, once for each "peanut." On "butter" throw both arms way up and to the right with fingers fully extended. Now go left with three step-close movements while manipulating the hands and fingers as before and throw arms up to the left on "butter."

For the next two lines, pretend you have a slice of bread on the upturned palm of one hand. Use the other hand as a knife (palm down-palm up movement) and move the knife over the bread rhythmically for four beats. Repeat the step-close lines above. On "JELLY" spread arms and legs out wide like for a jumping-jack exercise. Grin widely as you maintain that position.

The children will likely say, "Let's do it again!" Try going a little faster. Then pick up speed and volume equal to that of a cheer at an All-Star game.

Conversation with a Kite

Come back, come back, my runaway kite!

Come back and play with me!

I'm riding and gliding on whirl-away winds.

I'm going somewhere. Can't you see?

Where are you going, my beautiful kite,

flying so high in the sky?

I'm going to visit the lost balloons

That made little children cry.

When I held your string, oh my magical kite,

why did I feel the wind in my hand?

The wind is a taste of the sky, my young friend,

that I gave to a child of the land.

Bobbi Katz

The title indicates that this lengthy-lined composition is a dialogue between a child and his or her kite. There are many lovely images to enjoy. For choral speaking purposes, do not introduce this long rhyme until your choral group is ready.

The beat is steady, having four beats in the first line of each couplet and three beats in the second line. The only line where you must accelerate your speed to fit the words in, is line ten. Enunciate clearly so every word is heard.

The children can play the part of the child and you can be the kite; or, vice versa. Six rows of children could each recite one couplet. Or alternate two or three larger groups.

Run, Ducks, Run

Can you guess why the ducks

Are in such a big hurry;

What makes them all quack,

What makes them all scurry?

Why, of course— —they are running

To see Mrs. Skinner!

For the old farmer's wife

Has come with their dinner!

William Wise

Ducks are commonplace creatures on the farm. In verse one, Wise asks children unfamiliar with the farm, if they know why the ducks are in a hurry and scurry.

As the children recite these lines in questioning expression, they should raise their voices on "hurry" and "scurry." The answer returns exemplifying the quacking excitement of the ducks as they wobble hurriedly to get their fair share of dinner.

Any two groups or SOLOS could alternate every two lines. The teacher and children can each speak a verse; one group asking, the other answering.

Limericks

There was an Old Man with a beard,

Who said, "It is just as I feared! —

    Two Owls and a Hen,

    Four Larks and a Wren,

Have all built their nests in my beard!"

        There was a Young Lady whose chin

        Resembled the point of a pin;

           So she had it made sharp,

           And purchased a harp,

        And played several tunes with her chin.

A diner while dining at Crewe

Found a rather large mouse in his stew.

    Said the waiter, "Don't shout

    And wave it about,

Or the rest will be wanting one, too."

        There was a Young Maid who said, "Why

        Can't I look in my ear with my eye?

           If I give my mind to it,

           I'm sure I can do it,

        You never can tell till you try."

There was an Old Person of Ware,

Who rode on the back of a bear;

   When they said, "Does it trot?"

   He said: "Certainly not,

It's a Moppsikon, Floppsikon bear."

Edward Lear

Lear's limericks are found in every large children's anthology and in smaller volumes. Their humor belongs to the children. These five are my favorites but there are numerous others by Lear and other authors.

   Notice that the end words rhyme in lines one, two and five; and, lines three and four usually rhyme. The punctuation in these verses sometimes comes in unusual places. It is important that the sense of the sentence and the quotations stay intact. Because of the limerick style and content, use these verses with an experienced choral group, be that first, second, or third grade.

The Little Dreamer

A little boy was dreaming

Upon his mother's lap,

That the pins fell out of all the stars

And the stars fell into his cap.

So, when his dream was over,

What did this little boy do?

Why, he went and looked inside his cap

And found it was not true.

Old Rhyme

The type of dream described is loving and gentle, yet surprising. Work to attain all those moods in vocalization. You may experience other moods as you read this poem.

A soft to moderate volume seems fitting throughout. At the termination in the last two lines, raise the volume a bit. Faces should register surprise and perhaps wonderment.

Direct this selection in unison or, you might have two groups, one on each stanza.

A Centipede

A centipede was happy quite,

Until a frog in fun

Said, "Pray, which leg comes after which?"

This raised her mind to such a pitch,

She lay distracted in a ditch,

Considering how to run.

Unknown

Children identify easily with the teasing frog in this poem. If you can catch a centipede and introduce the creature in a large jar, the poem can have more meaning for the youngsters who have never seen one.

The end rhyming pattern in this composition is 2-6 and 3-4-5. To make sense, line two should be read: "Until a frog in fun said"—pause, "Pray"—pause, and continue. Draw special attention to the *wh* sound. Blow. To accentuate the speed with which a centipede runs, it is fun to speak line four fast, line five faster, and line six fastest. The word "considering" is perfect to propel the speed. Raise your voice one pitch higher for each of the last three lines.

Recite the poem in unison and use a strong SOLO on the quote. To break it down any further destroys the well-constructed climax and story line.

The Old Lady Who Swallowed a Fly

There was an old lady who swallowed a fly.
I don't know why she swallowed the fly;
Perhaps she'll die.

There was an old lady who swallowed a spider
That wiggled and jiggled and tickled inside her.
She swallowed the spider to catch the fly.
I don't know why she swallowed the fly;
Perhaps she'll die.

There was an old lady who swallowed a bird.
How absurd to swallow a bird!
She swallowed the bird to catch the spider
That wiggled and jiggled and tickled inside her.
She swallowed the spider to catch the fly.
I don't know why she swallowed the fly;
Perhaps she'll die.

There was an old lady who swallowed a cat.
Just think of that, to swallow a cat!
She swallowed the cat to catch the bird.
She swallowed the bird to catch the spider
That wiggled and jiggled and tickled inside her.
She swallowed the spider to catch the fly.
I don't know why she swallowed the fly;
Perhaps she'll die.

There was an old lady who swallowed a dog.
What a hog to swallow a dog!
She swallowed the dog to catch the cat.
She swallowed the cat to catch the bird.
She swallowed the bird to catch the spider
That wiggled and jiggled and tickled inside her.
She swallowed the spider to catch the fly.
I don't know why she swallowed the fly;
Perhaps she'll die.

There was an old lady who swallowed a goat.
She just opened her throat and swallowed the goat!
She swallowed the goat to catch the dog.
She swallowed the dog to catch the cat.
She swallowed the cat to catch the bird.
She swallowed the bird to catch the spider
That wiggled and jiggled and tickled inside her.
She swallowed the spider to catch the fly.
I don't know why she swallowed the fly;
Perhaps she'll die.

There was an old lady who swallowed a horse!
SHE'S DEAD OF COURSE!

Traditional

This is the only cumulative piece included in this collection because of length and repetition of lines. Any rhyme with repetitious lines can become very burdensome to recite. But the words of this selection are engaging.

After the children have the lines down pat, try six small groups, each pretending to be one of the creatures the old lady swallowed—the fly group, the spider group, etc. Every group says their own verse.

Or assign ALL on verse one with ALL on the first two lines, the "wiggled and jiggled and tickled" lines, plus the last two lines of each remaining stanza. The other lines can be delegated to SOLOS, the same SOLO repeating the line each time it occurs. It may help to write the names of the creatures in a column on the board in the sequence in which they are gobbled up. The change of groups and different sounds of the SOLOS will break the monotony of the repetition.

Use lots of appropriate verbal and facial expression, too. Rhyme "inside her" with "spider" by leaving out the *h* sound—inside-r. This is obviously not a number to use with beginners.

Nightfall

How fast the darkness

Overtakes the day

And blots out every memory

Of light and warmth and color

Then posts star sentinels

To show the way.

Emily Oszewski

Because of the imagery, Oszewski's "Nightfall" is more fitting for upper primary grades.

The word "overtakes" can be simply explained as "darkness chasing the day away." "Posts star sentinels," needs interpretation. Fairy tale picture books have familiarized children with sentinels or soldiers posted at the castle gate to protect the king and queen. Tell of the gentle darkness' concern to keep us safe by putting the stars out to guard us during the night.

Preferably, this selection should be taught outside—at camp after the campfire goes out or at an outdoor library storyhour. If taught in daylight hours inside, create your own darkness by pulling all the drapes and turning off all the lights. Have the children lay flat on their backs, close their eyes, and see their own twinklings of imagination while reciting the poem.

This is primarily a unison composition but you may prefer to arrange it for groups or SOLO performance. There is only one period but a natural pause occurs at the end of every two-line segment.

Awakening

I took an early morning winter walk

and stopped to rest beneath a snow-filled tree.

Everything was very still until

it woke and shook its bedding out on me.

Irene Zimmerman

The first two lines of this verse exemplify simple peace and calm. Interpret it vocally in that vein; however, if you are a jogger or exercise walker, you may wish to render the lines in a more vigorous fashion.

Line three leads to the climax. Start the line with medium-low volume and build to moderate-loud by the last word in the line. The poet prefaces the turning point by deliberately placing two rhyming words together. A marked pause after "still until" is suspenseful. Wide-eyed and smiling, the children can happily indulge in the tree's snow-shower.

This selection is most suited to unison delivery or as a SOLO number.

The Elephant Carries a Great Big Trunk

The elephant carries a great big trunk.

He never packs it with clothes;

It has no lock and it has no key,

But he takes it wherever he goes.

Anonymous

This riddle might not make sense to some of the youngest ones if you fail to clarify the meanings of the homonym, trunk. More of the older children will catch on through the context. Produce this rhyme smilingly with a humorous touch to your delivery.

Try a booming SOLO on line one, Group One on line two, and Group Two on line three. ALL finish the selection. If the children are in rows, invite each row to say a line. If the children need some movement time, have them line up shoulder to shoulder along the four sides of the room facing the center. Direct from one of the corners. Each side takes a line in rotation. Do not use this formation often, but children do like to do things differently now and then.

My Dog

His nose is short and scrubby;

His ears hang rather low;

And he always brings the stick back,

No matter how far you throw.

He gets spanked rather often

For things he shouldn't do,

Like lying-on-beds, and barking,

And eating up shoes when they're new.

He always wants to be going

Where he isn't supposed to go.

He tracks up the house when it's snowing—

Oh, puppy, I love you so.

Marchette Chute

This experiential poem allows for a wide range of affection and vigorous vocal expression. Establish a three-beat-per-line flow. Then the rhythm of the lines with extra syllables can be readily attacked. There should be no break or pause after the two lines without end punctuation; the dash after the word "snowing" requires a pause.

I automatically perform a little, lovable "tsk" sound at the dash by sucking the tip of my tongue against the gum of the upper teeth. Some children may have trouble producing this sound; others may confuse it with the clicking sound which would not be appropriate here. Absorb the "tsk" sound into the three beats of the last line. Unison recitation is impressive; however, other groupings are viable.

God, You Are Like...

God!

You are like the mother hen

that clucks to her chicks.

      May we listen to you.

You gather the chicks under your wings

to keep them safe and warm.

      May we be safe by you.

God!

You are like a shepherd

who watches and guards the sheep.

      May we be comforted.

You call the bleating animals

to come home.

      May we follow you.

God!

You are like the vinedresser

who digs, weeds and trims.

      May we help you work.

You pick the fruit

When it is ripe and juicy.

      May we have some to eat.

Rose Marie Anthony

Although easy to comprehend, this biblical paraphrasing is suitable for primary children well versed in choral speaking. This piece is poetic prose since the lines are not metered. It should flow like a prayer.

Because several of the sentences are lengthy, allow a quick breath at the end of the unpunctuated lines. More experienced groups can recite the lines through to the period without a break. If more capable SOLO children speak the long lines, remind them to take a good breath before starting.

Here are some possible arrangements. ALL speak the "God" and "May..." lines. Two groups can alternate the lengthy sentences, or six SOLOS can convey them in succession. Another alternative is to try one strong SOLO on the "God" and "May..." lines. The director should model those lines to give the SOLO the feel of it. ALL then vocalize the story lines. More simply, ask three groups to each say one little story. Clarify the words "bleating" and "vinedresser" for the children.

Merry Sunshine

"Good morning, Merry Sunshine,

How did you wake so soon,

You've scared the little stars away

And shined away the moon.

I saw you go to sleep last night

Before I ceased my playing;

How did you get 'way over there?

And where have you been staying?"

"I never go to sleep, dear child,

I just go round to see

My little children of the East,

Who rise and watch for me.

I waken all the birds and bees

And flowers on my way,

And now come back to see the child

Who stayed out late at play."

Anonymous

My rhyme collection for teaching primary poetry has had this selection in it for many years. It is a sensitive dialogue between a child and the sun. The child rambles on in verse one, asking questions and making observations about friend sun. In response, the sun answers gently, and to complete satisfaction, all the child's questions and lets the child know he is back again to befriend.

Ask the GIRLS to recite verse one; BOYS, verse two. Exchange. Use mixed groups. Teacher and children can also play each part. If you use division by lines, observe the punctuation. In other words, do not divide complete thoughts.

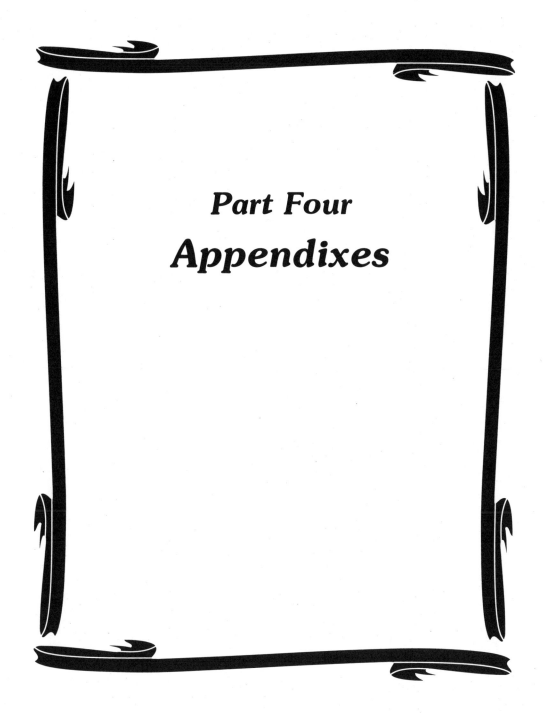

Part Four

Appendixes

Appendix A
Mother Goose Nursery
Rhyme Collections

Alderson, Brian, comp. *Cakes and Custard*. New York: William Morrow Company, 1975.

_____. *The Helen Oxenbury Nursery Rhyme Book*. Illus. by Helen Oxenbury. New York: William Morrow Company, 1986.

And So My Garden Grows. Illus. by Peter Spier. New York: Doubleday and Company, 1969.

As I Was Going Up and Down and Other Nursery Rhymes. Illus. by Nicola Bayley. New York: Macmillan Company, 1985.

B. B. Blacksheep and Company: A Collection of Favorite Nursery Rhymes. Illus. by Nick Butterworth. New York: Grosset and Dunlap, Inc., 1981.

Blake, Quentin, comp. and illus. *Quentin Blake's Nursery Rhyme Book*. New York: Harper and Row Company, 1983.

Blegvad, Lenore, comp. *The Parrot in the Garret*. Illus. by Erik Blegvad. New York: Atheneum, 1982.

_____. *This Little Pig-a-wig and Other Rhymes about Pigs*. New York: Atheneum, 1978.

Briggs, Raymond, comp. and illus. *Fee Fi Fo Fum: A Picture Book of Rhymes*. New York: Coward, McCann, Inc., 1964.

De Angeli, Marguerite, comp. and illus. *Marguerite De Angeli's Book of Nursery Rhymes and Mother Goose Rhymes*. New York: Doubleday and Company, Inc., 1954.

_____. *A Pocket Full of Posies: A Merry Mother Goose*. New York: Doubleday and Company, Inc., 1961.

de Paola, Tomie, comp. and illus. *Tomie de Paola's Mother Goose*. Putnam and Sons, Inc., 1985.

Dodson, Fitzhugh, comp. *I Wish I Had a Computer That Makes Waffles: Teaching Your Child with Modern Nursery Rhymes*. La Jolla, CA: Oak Tree Publications, 1978.

Fujikawa, Gyo, comp. and illus. *Gyo Fujikawa's Original Mother Goose*. New York: Grosset and Dunlap, Inc., 1968.

Hague, Michael, comp. and illus. *Mother Goose: A Collection of Classic Nursery Rhymes*. New York: Holt, Rinehart and Winston, 1984.

If Wishes Were Horses. Illus. by Susan Jeffers. New York: Dutton Company, 1979.

Kapp, Paul, comp. *A Cat Came Fiddling and Other Rhymes of Childhood*. Illus. by Irene Haas. New York: Harcourt, Brace and World, Inc., 1956.

Kent, Jack, comp. and illus. *Jack Kent's Merry Mother Goose*. New York: Golden Press, 1977.

Lines, Kathleen, comp. *Lavendar's Blue: A Book of Nursery Rhymes*. London: Oxford University Press, 1982.

Lobel, Arnold, comp. and illus. *The Random House Book of Mother Goose*. New York: Random House, Inc., 1986.

Low, Joseph, comp. *Mother Goose Riddle Rhymes*. New York: Harcourt, Brace and World, Inc., 1953.

Marshall, James, comp. and illus. *James Marshall's Mother Goose*. New York: Farrar, Straus and Giroux, Inc., 1979.

Mitchell, Susanne, comp. *The Larousse Book of Nursery Rhymes*. New York: Larousse and Company, 1984.

Mother Goose and Nursery Rhymes. Wood engravings by Phillip Reed. New York: Atheneum Publishers, 1963.

The Mother Goose Book. Illus. by Alice Provensen and Martin Provensen. New York: Random House, Inc., 1976.

Mother Goose Nursery Rhymes. Illus. by Arthur Rackham. New York: Viking Press, 1975.

Mother Goose or the Old Nursery Rhymes. Illus. by Kate Greenaway. London: Warne Company, n.d.

The Mother Goose Treasury. Illus. by Raymond Briggs. New York: Dell Publishing Company, 1986.

One Misty Moisty Morning: Rhymes from Mother Goose. Illus. by Mitchell Miller. New York: Farrar, Straus and Giroux, Inc., 1971.

Opie, Iona, and Peter Opie, comps. *The Oxford Nursery Rhyme Book*. Early woodcuts by Joan Hassell. New York: Oxford University Press, 1955.

Opie, Iona Archibald, comp. *Tail Feathers from Mother Goose: The Opie Rhyme Book*. Boston: Little, Brown and Company, 1988.

Ormerod, Jan, comp. *Rhymes around the Day*. New York: Lothrop, Lee and Shepard, 1983.

Over the Moon. Illus. by Charlotte Voke. New York: C. N. Potter, distributed by Crown Publishers, 1985.

Patz, Nancy, comp. *Moses Supposes His Toeses Are Roses and 7 Other Silly Old Rhymes*. San Diego, CA: Harcourt, Brace and Jovanovich, 1983.

Pooley, Sarah, comp. *A Day of Rhymes*. New York: Knopf, distributed by Random House, 1987.

Rockwell, Anne, comp. and illus. *Gray Goose and Gander and Other Mother Goose Rhymes*. New York: T. Y. Crowell Company, 1980.

Sewal, Roberta, ed. *The Golden Goose and Other Favorites*. Illus. by Leslie L. Brooke. New York: Avenel Books, n.d.

Sing a Song of Sixpense. Illus. by Randolph Caldecott. New York: Barron's, 1987.

Szekeres, Cyndy, comp. and illus. *Cyndy Szekeres' Mother Goose Rhymes*. New York: Golden Press, 1987.

Tom, Tom, the Piper's Son. Illus. by Paul Galdone. New York: McGraw-Hill Book Co., 1964.

Tripp, Wallace, comp. and illus. *Granfa Grig Had a Pig and Other Rhymes without Reason*. Boston: Little, Brown and Company, 1976.

Tucker, Nicholas, comp. *Mother Goose Lost*. Illus. by Trevor Stubly. New York: Thomas Y. Crowell Company, 1971.

Watson, Jane Werner, comp. *The Golden Mother Goose: 163 Favorites*. Illus. by Alice Provensen and Martin Provensen. New York: Golden Press, 1948.

Weigle, Oscar, comp. *A Treasury of Mother Goose*. Illus. by Harold Berson. New York: Grosset & Dunlap Publishers, 1967.

Werner, Jane, ed. *The Giant Golden Mother Goose*. New York: Golden Press, 1970.

Wildsmith, Brian, comp. and illus. *Brian Wildsmith's Mother Goose: A Collection of Nursery Rhymes*. New York: Franklin Watts, Inc., 1964.

Wyndham, Robert, ed. *Chinese Mother Goose Rhymes*. Cleveland, OH: World Publishing Company, 1968.

Appendix B
Anthologies and Poetry Collections

Note: When choosing choral selections, use books both of the past and the present. This bibliography is but a sampling of the books available.

Aldis, Dorothy. *All Together: A Child's Treasury of Verse*. New York: G. P. Putnam's Sons, 1952.

_____. *Quick As a Wink*. New York: G. P. Putnam's Sons, 1960.

Alexander, Martha, sel. *Poems and Prayers for the Very Young*. New York: Random House, 1973.

Arbuthnot, May Hill, and Sheldon L. Root, Jr., comps. *Time for Poetry*. 3rd ed. Glenview, IL: Scott, Foresman & Company, 1961.

Austin, Mary C., and Queenie B. Mills, comps. *The Sound of Poetry*. Boston: Allyn & Bacon, Inc., 1964.

Baines, Murphy Rowan, comp. *One, Two, Buckle My Shoe: A Book of Counting Rhymes*. New York: Simon and Schuster, 1987.

Barrows, Marjorie, comp. *One Hundred Best Poems for Boys and Girls*. New York: Core Collection Books, 1976.

Behn, Harry. *Crickets and Bullfrogs and Whispers of Thunder*. Sel. by Lee Bennett Hopkins. San Diego, CA: Harcourt, Brace and Jovanovich, 1984.

_____. *The Golden Hive*. New York: Harcourt, Brace and World, Inc., 1966.

Bennett, Rowena. *The Day Is Dancing*. Chicago: Follett Company, 1948.

Bodecker, N. M. *Snowman Sniffles and Other Verse*. New York: Atheneum, 1983.

Brooks, Gwendolyn. *Bronzeville Boys and Girls*. New York: Harper and Row Publishers, 1956.

Brown, Helen A., sel. *Let's Read-Together Poems*. Evanston, IL: Row, Peterson Company, 1949.

Childcraft Poems and Rhymes. Chicago: Field Enterprises Educational Corporation, 1971. (Childcraft, any year)

Chute, Marchette Gaylord. *Around and About*. New York: Dutton Company, 1957.

_____. *Rhymes about the Country*. New York: Macmillan Company, 1941.

Ciardi, John. *Doodle Soup*. Boston: Houghton Mifflin Company, 1985.

Cole, Joanna, sel. *A New Treasury of Children's Poetry*. New York: Doubleday and Company, 1984.

Cole, William, comp. *A Book of Animal Poems*. New York: Viking Press, 1973.

_____. *A Boy Named Mary Jane and Other Silly Verse*. New York: Franklin Watts, Inc., 1977.

_____. *Oh, Such Foolishness*. Philadelphia: Lippincott Company, 1978.

_____. *Oh, That's Ridiculous*. New York: Viking Press, 1972.

_____. *Pick Me Up: A Book of Short, Short Poems*. New York: Macmillan Company, 1972.

De la Mare, Walter. *Peacock Pie*. New York: A. A. Knopf, Inc., 1961.

_____. *Rhymes and Verses: Collected Poems for Children*. New York: H. Holt and Company, 1927.

deRegniers, Beatrice Schenk, sel. *Sing a Song of Popcorn: Every Child's Book of Poems*. (Revised edition of *Poems Children Will Sit Still For*.) New York: Scholastic, Inc., 1988.

_____. *The Way I Feel—Sometimes*. New York: Clarion Books, 1988.

Farber, Norma, and Myra Cohn Livingston, comps. *These Small Stones*. New York: Harper and Row Publishers, 1987.

Farjeon, Eleanor. *Eleanor Farjeon's Poems for Children*. Philadelphia: J. B. Lippincott Company, 1951.

Fisher, Aileen. *Cricket in a Thicket*. New York: Charles Scribner's Sons, 1963.

_____. *The House of a Mouse*. New York: Harper and Row Publishers, 1988.

_____. *In the Woods, In the Meadow, In the Sky*. New York: Charles Scribner's Sons, 1965.

_____. *Out in the Dark and Daylight*. New York: Harper and Row Publishers, 1980.

_____. *Runny Days, Sunny Days*. New York: Abelard-Schuman, 1933.

_____. *Up the Windy Hill*. New York: Abelard-Schuman, 1933.

Frost, Robert. *You Come Too*. New York: Holt, Rinehart and Winston Company, 1959.

Fujikawa, Gyo, comp. and illus. *A Child's Book of Poems*. New York: Grosset and Dunlap Company, 1983.

Fyleman, Rose. *Fairies and Chimneys*. New York: Doubleday and Company, Inc., 1920.

_____. *Pipe and Drum*. Philadelphia: Frederick A. Stokes, 1940.

Hearn, Michael Patrick, sel. *Breakfast, Books and Dreams*. New York: Frederick Warne Company, 1981.

Hoberman, Mary Ann. *The Raucous Awk — A Menagerie of Poems*. New York: Viking Press, 1973.

Hopkins, Lee Bennett, comp. *And God Bless Me: Prayers, Lullabies and Dream-poems*. New York: Knopf, distributed by Random House, Inc., 1982.

_____. *Best Friends*. New York: Harper and Row Publishers, 1986.

_____. *By Myself*. New York: Thomas Y. Crowell Company, 1980.

_____. *The City Spreads Its Wings*. New York: Franklin Watts, Inc., 1970.

_____. *Click, Rumble, Roar: Poems about Machines*. New York: Thomas Y. Crowell Company, 1987.

_____. *Dinosaurs*. San Diego, CA: Harcourt, Brace and Jovanovich, 1987.

_____. *Girls Can Too!* New York: Franklin Watts, Inc., 1972.

_____. *Surprises*. New York: Harper and Row Company, 1984.

Hughes, Langston. *Don't You Turn Back*. Sel. by Lee Bennett Hopkins. New York: A. A. Knopf, Inc., 1969.

_____. *The Dream Keeper and Other Poems*. New York: Knopf, distributed by Random House, 1960.

Ichikawa, Satomi. *Here a Little Child I Stand*. New York: Philomel Books, 1985.

Illustrated Poems for Children: A Special Collection. Illus. by Krystyna Stasniak. Chicago: Children's Press, 1984.

Itse, Elizabeth M., comp. *Hey, Bug! And Other Poems about Little Things*. New York: American Heritage Press, 1972.

Jacobs, Leland B., ed. *Arithmetic in Verse and Rhyme*. Scarsdale, NY: Garrard Publishing Company, 1971.

_____. *Just around the Corner*. New York: Holt, Rinehart and Winston, 1964.

_____. *Poetry for Space Enthusiasts*. Scarsdale, NY: Garrard Publishing Company, 1971.

Katz, Bobbi. *Poems for Small Friends*. New York: Random House, 1989.

_____. *Upside Down and Inside Out*. New York: Franklin Watts, Inc., 1973.

Kennedy, X. J., comp. *Knock at a Star*. Boston: Little, Brown and Company, 1982.

Kuskin, Karla. *Dogs and Dragons, Trees and Dreams*. New York: Harper and Row, 1980.

Larrick, Nancy, comp. *Bring Me All of Your Dreams*. New York: M. Evans, 1980.

_____. *When the Dark Comes Dancing*. New York: Philomel Books, 1983.

Lear, Edward. *The Complete Book of Nonsense*. New York: Dodd, Mead and Company, 1912.

_____. *Nonsense Song*. New York: Frederick Warne and Company, Ltd., n.d.

Lewis, Richard, comp. *Miracles: Poems by Children of the English Speaking World*. New York: Simon and Schuster Company, 1966.

Lindsay, Vachel. *Johnny Appleseed and Other Poems*. New York: Macmillan Company, 1913.

Livingston, Myra Cohn, comp. *Christmas Poems*. New York: Holiday House, 1984.

_____. *I Like You, If You Like Me*. New York: Margaret K. McElderry Books, 1987.

_____. *Poems for Jewish Holidays*. New York: Holiday House, 1986.

_____. *O Sliver of Liver*. New York: Atheneum, 1979.

_____. *Thanksgiving Poems*. New York: Holiday House, 1985.

_____. *Valentine Poems*. New York: Holiday House, 1987.

_____. *Whispers and Other Poems*. New York: Harcourt, Brace and World, 1958.

McCord, David. *Every Time I Climb a Tree.* Boston: Little, Brown and Company, 1925.

_____. *Far and Few.* Boston: Little, Brown and Company, 1952.

_____. *The Star in the Pail.* Boston: Little, Brown and Company, 1975.

Merriam, Eve. *Blackberry Ink.* New York: William Morrow Company, 1985.

_____. *Catch a Little Rhyme.* New York: Atheneum, 1967.

_____. *Fresh Paint: New Poems by Eve Merriam.* New York: Macmillan Company, 1986.

_____. *Halloween ABC.* New York: Macmillan Company, 1987.

Milne, Alan Alexander. *Now We Are Six.* New York: E. P. Dutton and Company, 1927.

Moore, Lilian, comp. *Catch Your Breath: A Book of Shivery Poems.* Champaign, IL: Garrard Publishing Company, 1973.

_____. *I Feel the Same Way.* New York: Atheneum, 1967.

_____. *To See the World Afresh.* New York: Atheneum, 1974.

Nash, Ogden. *Custard and Company: Poems by Ogden Nash.* Sel. by Quentin Blake. Boston: Little, Brown and Company, 1980.

_____. *The Moon Is Shining Bright as Day.* Philadelphia: Lippincott, 1953.

O'Neill, Mary. *Hailstones and Halibut Bones.* New York: Doubleday and Company, Inc., 1961.

Prelutsky, Jack. *Gopher in the Garden.* New York: Macmillan Company, 1986.

_____. *The New Kid on the Block.* New York: Greenwillow Books, 1984.

_____. *My Parents Think I'm Sleeping.* New York: Greenwillow Books, 1985.

_____. *The Random House Book of Poetry for Children.* New York: Random House, 1983.

_____. *Read Aloud Rhymes for the Very Young.* New York: Alfred A. Knopf, Inc., 1986.

_____. *Zoo Doings: Animal Poems.* New York: Greenwillow Books, 1983.

Richards, Laura E. *Tirra Lirra Rhymes Old and New.* Boston: Little, Brown and Company, 1902.

Ridlon, Marci. *That Was Summer.* Chicago: Follett Publishing Company, 1969.

Rosenblum, Joseph. *Silly Verse and Even Worse.* New York: Sterling Publishing Company, 1979.

Rosetti, Christina. *Goblin Market*. New York: Franklin Watts, Inc., 1970.

_____. *Sing Song*. New York: Macmillan Company, 1924.

Sandburg, Carl. *Early Moon*. New York: Harcourt, Brace and World, Inc., 1930.

_____. *Rainbows Are Made*. Sel. by Lee Bennett Hopkins. New York: Harcourt, Brace, and Jovanovich Publishers, 1982.

Silverstein, Shel. *A Light in the Attic*. New York: Harper and Row Publishers, 1981.

Spilka, Arnold. *A Lion I Can Do Without*. New York: Henry Z. Walck, Inc., 1964.

_____. *A Rumbudgin of Nonsense*. New York: Charles Scribner's Sons, 1970.

Stevenson, Robert Louis. *A Child's Garden of Verses*. Cleveland, OH: World Publishing Company, 1946.

Tashjian, Virginia A. *Juba This and Juba That*. Boston: Little, Brown and Company, 1969.

Tripp, Wallace, comp. *A Great Big Ugly Man Came Up and Tied His Horse to Me: A Book of Nonsense Verse*. Boston: Little, Brown and Company, 1973.

Untermeyer, Louis, ed. *The Golden Book of Poems for the Very Young*. New York: Golden Press, 1971.

_____. *Poems*. New York: Golden Press, 1959.

_____. *Rainbow in the Sky*. San Diego, CA: Harcourt, Brace and Jovanovich, 1985.

Wise, William. *All on a Summer's Day*. New York: Pantheon, 1971.

Zolotow, Charlotte. *All That Sunlight*. New York: Harper and Row Publishers, 1967.

Appendix C
Related References

Behn, Harry. *Chrysalis: Concerning Children and Poetry*. New York: Harcourt, Brace and Jovanovich, 1968.

Brewton, John E., G. Meredith Blackburn III, and Lorraine A. Blackburn, comps. *Index to Poetry for Children and Young People*. New York: H. W. Wilson Company, 1984.

Eastman, Max. *The Enjoyment of Poetry*. New York: Charles Scribner's Sons, Inc., 1951.

Green, Percy B. *A History of Nursery Rhymes*. Detroit, MI: Singing Tree (Gale Research Company), 1968.

Halliwell-Phillipps, James O. *Popular Rhymes and Nursery Tales: A Sequel to the Nursery Rhymes of England*. Detroit, MI: Singing Tree (Gale Research Company), 1968.

Haviland, Virginia, and Margaret Coughlan, comps. *Yankee Doodle's Literacy Sampler of Prose, Poetry, & Pictures*. New York: Thomas Y. Crowell Company, 1974.

Hopkins, Lee Bennett. *Pass the Poetry, Please.* rev. ed. New York: Harper and Row Publishers, 1987.

Huber, Miriam Blanton. *Story and Verse for Children*. New York: Macmillan Company, 1965.

Huck, Charlotte S., Susan Hepler, and Janet Hickman. *Children's Literature in the Elementary School*. 4th ed. New York: Holt, Rinehart & Winston, Inc., 1987.

Jacobs, Leland, ed. *Using Literature with Young Children.* New York: Teacher's College Press, 1965.

Johnson, Edna, Evelyn Sickels, and Frances Clarke Sayers. *Anthology of Children's Literature.* 4th ed. Boston, MA: Houghton Mifflin Company, 1970.

Larrick, Nancy, ed. *Somebody Turned on a Tap in These Kids.* New York: Delacorte Press, 1971.

Meeker, Alice M. *Enjoying Literature with Children.* Indianapolis, IN: Odyssey (Bobbs Merrill Company), 1969.

Opie, Iona, and Peter Opie, comps. *The Lore and Language of School Children.* New York: Oxford University Press, 1959.

_____. *The Original Mother Goose's Melody, As First Issued by John Newbery, of London, about A.D. 1760.* Detroit, MI: Singing Tree (Gale Research Company), 1969.

Ribner, Irving, and Harry Morris. *Poetry: A Critical and Historical Introduction.* Glenview, IL: Scott, Foresman and Company, 1962.

Sanders, Thomas E. *The Discovery of Poetry.* Glenview, IL: Scott, Foresman and Company, 1967.

Sutherland, Zena, Dianne L. Monson, and May Hill Arbuthnot. *Children and Books.* Glenview, IL: Scott, Foresman and Company, 1986.

Witucke, Virginia. *Poetry in the Elementary School.* Dubuque, IA: William C. Brown Company Publishers, 1970.

Appendix D
Poet Index

Appendix E
First-Line Index

About the Author

Rose Marie Anthony, a Racine Dominican sister, is a library coordinator in a Milwaukee, Wisconsin, elementary school. She taught primary grades for many years and also served as a library services director for children in a public library for eight and one half years. She has taught summer sessions in children's literature at the college level and is working on curriculum for classes in the art of choral speaking.

Index